P9-DWS-289

Names,
Not Just Numbers,
Facing Global AIDS and World Hunger

Donald E. Messer

Speaker's Corner

Golden, Colorado

Library of Congress Control Number: 2010931652

Printed on recycled paper in Canada by Friesens Corp.

0 9 8 7 6 5 4 3 2 1

Design by Jack Lenzo
Cover image © Shutterstock | Lucian Coman

Speaker's Corner Books
An imprint of Fulcrum Publishing, Inc.
4690 Table Mountain Drive, Suite 100
Golden, Colorado 80403
800-992-2908 • 303-277-1623
www.speakerscornerbooks.com

Dedicated to

Suzanne Calvin

Pamela Merrill

Marla Petrini

Claudia Svarstad

Herb and Laura May Bacon

and all the ambassadors and friends of the Center for the

Church and Global AIDS, who with Mother Teresa believe that

"In this life we cannot do great things. We can only do small

things with great love."

Contents

Introduction

Bombarded by staggering statistics describing the number of people facing the threats of world hunger and global AIDS (acquired immune deficiency syndrome), individuals often feel overwhelmed by the magnitude of the crisis and bewildered as to what they can do to make a difference. Rarely do these figures have more than a passing impact on the individual mind or heart. The danger of writing a book probing these topics is that further analysis can lead to paralysis rather than prompting the type of attitudinal change and personal action I passionately hope to encourage. The world must confront three powerful and perplexing pandemics: world hunger, global AIDS, and human indifference.

People are more inclined to respond to stories than to statistics, faces rather than facts, and names rather than numbers. When I speak to audiences across the United States and in other countries, what triggers the imagination and touches the heartstrings are not abstract statistics but portraits of people struggling to conquer hunger and disease. In this book, therefore, I have tried to focus on the faces of people on the front lines of illness and malnutrition, as well as provide the statistical, analytical, and political dimensions of world hunger and global AIDS. Numbers are not unimportant, but it is the names—the up close and personal relationships—that potentially enable the reader to understand and identify with these crises of humanity.

Linking World Hunger and Global AIDS

The invitation to write this book was extended by Bob Baron, publisher of Fulcrum Publishing, following a lecture I presented at the annual George S. McGovern Conference at Dakota Wesleyan University that linked world hunger and global AIDS. This volume is designed to be a logical sequel to two of my earlier books, *Breaking the Conspiracy of Silence: Christian Churches and the Global AIDS Crisis* (Fortress, 2004) and *Ending Hunger Now: A Challenge to Persons of Faith* (Fortress, 2005), the latter cowritten with former senators George S. McGovern and Bob Dole. What particularly distinguishes this book is connecting hunger and AIDS, providing compelling narratives of people struggling with these pandemics—both the malnourished and those infected and affected by HIV (human immunodeficiency virus)/AIDS.

Due to a heavy speaking schedule prompted by these two books, and my international work through the Center for the Church and Global AIDS, completion of this volume was delayed. In retrospect, however, this proved beneficial in two ways. First, I was able to gain considerable firsthand knowledge of the crises through my engagements in Zambia, Kenya, South Africa, Malawi, Barbados, Mexico, Malaysia, India, Singapore, Thailand, Bangladesh, Sri Lanka, and Burma. Second, revised statistics from UNAIDS (the joint United Nations program on HIV/AIDS) in late 2007 significantly reduced estimates of the number of people infected with HIV from over 40 million to 33 million. In reality, no fewer people were infected than previously, but some feared that better statistical accuracy might diminish public concern and commitment even further than previously. My contention, however, is that focusing on names, not just numbers, faces, not just facts, holds the greater possibility of overcoming human indifference.

Ironically, while this book focuses on names and personal identities, the real names of people living with HIV and AIDS often had to be disguised because the people infected risk severe stigmatization and demeaning discrimination.

Keeping Up to Date

The size of this book has been a special challenge, since writing succinctly but comprehensively is required in this book series. Readers seeking to keep up to date on statistics, trends, and developments are encouraged to view websites such as UNAIDS (www .unaids.org), the UN World Food Programme (www .wfp.org), or my own website (www.churchandglobal aids.org).

Expressing Gratitude

What appears in print always remains the responsibility of the author, but writing a book requires the assistance of many people without whose invaluable help the manuscript could never have been completed. Particularly, I want to thank Megan Armstrong, coordinator for the Center for the Church and Global AIDS, for her timely research contributions and persistent encouragement. Appreciation also is due to the able assistance of Margaret Mahan, Ryan Beeman Weiland, and Andre Roux, along with the vision, patience, and support of the editors at Fulcrum Publishing.

As always, my wife, Bonnie J. Messer, has been a companion not only in the writing, but more importantly in the experiences that contributed to the writing of this manuscript. Besides accompanying me on many international travels and speaking engagements, she has steadfastly urged me to write and to share my dreams for a more humane planet. A bit reluctantly, but quite generously, she realizes that my retirement from a lifetime of serving as a college and seminary president is proving to be a new journey of nearly full-time service in quest of an AIDS-free and hunger-free world. Together, we envision and work toward a better world for our grandchildren and future generations.

Around the world HIV and AIDS impacts the most impoverished, whether they are in southern Africa, southern Asia, or the southern United States.

One evening when I preached in a rural South Carolina African American church a few steps from a cotton field in full bloom, five people self-identified themselves as HIV positive, four of whom were women. Between the ages of forty and sixty, each shared their stories of how difficult it was to get medication and food, pay for transportation to the clinic, and live with the stigma associated with the disease. I have heard the same stories from people in South Africa and South India.

HIV and AIDS are escalating in rural America. In western Colorado women comprise about 30 percent of those infected with HIV. In rural Nebraska people needing antiretroviral drugs have been lingering on waiting lists. In South Carolina somebody had to die before a new person could get the needed medicine. In 2010 it was sometimes easier to get US government pills in Namibia than Nebraska, or South Africa than South Carolina!

Chapter One
Beyond Nameless Numbers

Every three seconds a person dies somewhere in the world due to poverty—that means 8 million nameless people a year. Over 1 billion people go to bed hungry every night.[1] Yesterday some 30,000 people died from malnutrition and hunger, of which 18,000 were children. Today an estimated 6,000 people died from AIDS, 5,000 from tuberculosis, and 3,000 from malaria. Last year at least 2.1 million people died of AIDS and almost 3 million more became infected with HIV. *And most people don't give a shit!*

The Profanity of Needless Deaths
In fact, most readers will not remember a single statistic outlined above, but they will remember I used profanity. As a clergyman, if I dare say this in a speech or sermon, people are more upset by my bad language than they are that women, men, and children are dying needlessly around the globe.

The moral, religious, and political scandal of people dying from hunger and diseases in a world with sufficient food and medicine for everyone hardly causes a ripple in the consciousness of most people. We may find dirty words offensive, but the dirty deeds of permitting hunger and disease to run rampant across an affluent globe barely prompts a protest.

Who Cares about the Millennium Development Goals?
When I speak to most audiences in the United States

and mention the Millennium Development Goals, they respond with a vacant stare. It is not clear whether anybody cares about these international objectives, or whether they have simply never heard of them, or if it is some combination of disinterest and devaluation.

In September 2000, in an act endorsed by all the countries of the world, the United Nations adopted the Millennium Declaration. In a dramatic decision, the world's 147 heads of state affirmed eight major goals to eliminate extreme poverty, disease, and environmental degradation, outlining strategies and timetables for overcoming the conditions that entrap people in virtual economic slavery their entire lives.

Economist Jeffrey Sachs at Columbia University invites us to imagine an economic ladder with the lower rungs representing subsistence agriculture; the next, moving upward, symbolizing light manufacturing; and the top rungs denoting high-tech and professional services. "Roughly 1 billion people around the world, one-sixth of humanity," notes Sachs, are "too ill, hungry, or destitute even to get a foot on the first rung of the development ladder."[2] These are the planet's poorest of the poor, those condemned to lifelong extreme poverty, women, men, and children who struggle to survive each and every day.

The eight Millennium Development Goals (or MDGs) provide a bold and hopeful agenda toward which nations, nongovernmental organizations, faith-based communities, and individuals are encouraged to strive. The first seven goals envision

drastic reductions in poverty, disease, and environmental degradation, while the eighth is a call for a
global partnership to achieve these objectives.

The MDGs articulate what once were considered simply utopian dreams but now are viewed as
practical political possibilities. Scientists, economists,
and international leaders now deem these hopes as
not beyond human reach but potentially within our
grasp, if there is sufficient political will and sustained
human compassion to systematically pursue them. In
summary, the MDGs challenge us to:

1. **Eradicate extreme poverty and hunger**—By 2015,
   reduce by half the proportion of people whose
   income is less than a dollar a day and the number
   who suffer from hunger.

2. **Achieve universal primary education**—By 2015,
   ensure that both girls and boys everywhere have
   access to a basic education.

3. **Promote gender equality and empower women**—
   Focus particularly on eliminating gender inequality
   in primary and secondary education, preferably by
   2005 but no later than 2015.

4. **Reduce child mortality**—Between 1990 and 2015,
   cut the mortality rate of children under five by
   two-thirds.

5. **Improve maternal health**—Between 1990 and 2015,
   cut the mortality rate of mothers by three-quarters.

6. **Combat HIV/AIDS, malaria, and other diseases**—
   Halt and begin to prevent the spread of disease by
   2015.

7. **Ensure environmental sustainability**—Integrate sustainable development programs and processes, overcome the loss of environmental resources, halve by 2015 the proportion of people without safe drinking water and sanitation, and improve significantly the lives of at least 100 million slum dwellers by 2020.

8. **Develop a global partnership for development**—Create new frameworks for dealing with finances, trade, debt relief, affordable medicine, and technology.

On September 11, 2001, just about a year after the MDGs were embraced, terrorists struck the United States and the political and international landscape changed drastically. Fear triumphed over hope, and suspicion replaced compassion. Instead of reaching out across the oceans to provide neighborly help to the forgotten indigent of the world, we instead were encouraged to look for suspicious activity among our next-door neighbors lest they be disguised as terrorists waiting to strike. As we mourned the tragic death of some 3,000 people killed in New York, Pennsylvania, and Washington, DC, on that fateful day, we chose to forget that *every day* 10,000 Africans die from preventable malnutrition and disease.

Statistics: Numbers without Tears

Hunger, AIDS, poverty, sexism, racism, and indifference are all inextricably linked in a web of discouraging truths. Some 1.2 billion people across our globe are hungry. More than 16,000 children die from hunger-related causes every day. Of the 33.4 million people living with HIV/AIDS, 68 percent live in Sub-Saharan Africa.[3] Seventy-six percent of all AIDS-related deaths and 68 percent of new infections last year occurred in that region (1.7 million in 2006, compared to 2.2 million in 2005). Areas of Africa and other developing countries have seen a drastic reduction in food production due to decreased harvesters, as many of those countries' young men and women are too sick from HIV or AIDS (or have already died) to grow and harvest food. Children are the most affected by these terrible numbers, as they are impacted in many ways. In 2005, about 10.1 million children died before they reached their fifth birthday.[4] The children who do live past their fifth birthday are in many cases becoming orphans due to the AIDS virus.

Statistics are simply nameless numbers or, as the African proverb proclaims, statistics are numbers without tears. We simply fail to identify with numbers; they are nonpersons in our minds and hearts. Facts without faces do not evoke within us a sense of political commitment or personal compassion. As the poet, playwright, and statesman Archibald MacLeish once said, "We are deluged with facts, but we have lost or are losing our human ability to feel them." He argued that "knowledge without feeling is not knowledge and can lead only to public irresponsibility and indifference, and conceivably to ruin."

Personally, I find it transformative to reframe statistics into stories and visualize faces with the facts. By giving names to numbers, I not only remember my sisters and brothers in need, but discover a new sensitivity in my soul and new hope in my heart. Instead of just talking abstractly about hunger, disease, and poverty, let me introduce you to some people I have encountered on my journey.

Khin Myo Bu in a Thailand Garbage Dump

During a visit to Thailand, I had the most heart-wrenching experience. A friend invited me to go with him to visit a person living with AIDS. When I said yes, I did not realize that, in a few minutes, we would be visiting a woman dying of AIDS in the garbage-filled slums of Chiang Mai.

The typical visitor to Chiang Mai sees only beautiful landscapes, magnificent golf courses, exotic elephant camps, glitzy nightclubs, and busy night markets filled with incredible bargains. But behind the glitter of this cosmopolitan city are more than twenty garbage dumps where people struggle to eke out a living. There, amid a mountain of rubbish, are tin shacks stuck together in the crudest fashion. Ducking under the rough edge of a tin roof, I saw beneath a mosquito net a twenty-eight-year-old mother dying from AIDS. With bones nearly protruding through her gnarled skin, her once lovely face was now disfigured grotesquely. She was barely surviving, unable to drink or eat.

The heat, stench, and dirt were unbelievable, but people live and raise families in these wretched circumstances. The young neighborhood women I met make $2 a day by digging through the trash for plastic and tin cans for recycling. This woman with AIDS was a refugee from totalitarian Burma (Myanmar), where $2 a day is more than many professionals earn. Her husband had already died of AIDS, and now she was lying emaciated under a mosquito net in a squalid hut. Beside her were her two malnourished sons, ages seven and five, about to be orphaned, with absolutely nowhere to go.

My Thai friend Reverend Sanan Wutti of the Church of Christ in Thailand, however, had long ago committed himself to an AIDS ministry. So he talked with the neighbor women about the family's basic needs: food, school fees for the children, supplies for incontinence, rubber gloves, literally everything. He returned later that day with these items, but it was too late for Khin Myo Bu; she died that night in the garbage armpits of one of the world's most popular tourist meccas.

But even as we gathered food and supplies, the more urgent concern was what would happen to these impoverished little boys. No hope existed that they could return to grandparents or loved ones in Burma. Later that day we visited an orphanage in Chiang Mai—an oasis of hope founded by a Canadian woman—and explored the possibility of transferring the boys there after their mother died.

Paula Gill outside a Barbados Church

In contrast, I met Paula Gill outside a church door in Bridgetown, Barbados. It was just before World

AIDS Day (December 1), and I had just finished leading a workshop and preaching to a large congregation about the teaching of Jesus to feed the hungry, clothe the naked, and visit the sick. As I was greeting congregants at the outside door, an attractively dressed woman asked to speak with me privately when the others had left. Afraid she would draw attention from others mingling outside, she asked if she could speak confidentially inside the sanctuary.

Dressed in colorful Caribbean clothing, with an attractive turbanlike hat on her head, Paula stood in front of me with a baby in her arms and another child holding her hand. With embarrassment she began to speak. "My husband has died from AIDS, and I am HIV positive. I'm working, but I don't have enough money to care for the children. They need food, and the baby has no diapers. Can you find me some help?"

Infected by her husband, this faithful churchgoing woman felt terribly alone, uncertain what people were saying about her and her family. When you are poor, hungry, and HIV positive, you know that other people are not anxious to be with you; in fact, you are likely to experience stigmatization and discrimination. Paula sought confidential assistance, fearing that if others knew of her situation they would reject her presence, even at church.

Even as I sought to get her some immediate assistance, echoing through my mind were the lyrics of a song sung by an AIDS support group in the musical *Rent*. They were words that would have resonated in Paula's heart: "Will I lose my dignity? Will someone care? Will I wake tomorrow from this nightmare?"

William Kahangi Hawking on the Streets of Kenya

When I met William Kahangi, he appeared to be a healthy forty-year-old man, full of energy and enthusiasm. Walking down the streets of Eldoret, Kenya, he greeted my physician friend with joy: "Professor, Professor, so good to see you." Turning to me, he exclaimed, "The good doctor saved my life." As my humble medical friend slipped into a restaurant, William declared, "If it had not been for him, I would now be dead."

I stopped and asked some questions, and William was eager to answer them. He told me he was at death's door, unable to walk or do anything else. Once he had been tested and learned he was HIV positive, his wife, family, and friends all left him. As the disease flourished, he lost his ability to earn an income as a hawker selling clothes on a Kenya street. Who wants to buy clothes from a sickly gaunt guy with open, protruding sores oozing pus? Without any income, he had no way to maintain himself or purchase food, much less medicine. His situation continued to deteriorate until he was hospitalized, and he was praying that the angel of death would rescue him.

Instead, an unexpected volunteer angel of life, Dr. Joseph Mamlin, a retired medical professor from Indiana University, came to his bedside and offered him prescriptions of medicine and nutrition that eventually restored both his body and spirit. Now he was back at his chosen work as a hawker, a productive citizen of Kenya. Eager to tell his story to anyone who will listen, William encourages people to get tested and to take advantage of the antiretroviral AIDS medicines that are now available thanks to the US and Kenyan governments.

Mary Mbeki on an Airplane

Getting settled into yet another seat on yet another airplane at some ungodly hour of the morning in Los Angeles, I greeted the young woman beside me. She welcomed me with a smile, and I asked her where she was headed. She introduced herself as Mary Mbeki and said she was heading home to South Africa. In the ensuing conversation, I indicated I had been to Johannesburg two years before, as I was involved in the struggle against HIV and AIDS.

She responded by saying she was going home to be with her sister Zoe, age twenty-seven, the mother of a nine-year-old. Zoe's T-cell count was falling into the low two hundreds, and Mary needed to get home to help determine how to care for her. I inquired whether antiretrovirals were available for Zoe, but Mary reported that she hesitated to get her on medicine with severe side effects that she would have to take for a lifetime. I argued that not to medicate was too dangerous, but she reminded me that the medicine they get is not always the same as in the United States and could be too toxic for her sister, who didn't always get enough good nutrition.

Forgotten were my early morning blues and self-pity as I listened to her tell me what it is like to be a South African and feel "like every other friend has HIV." She shook her head sadly, saying, "I'm tired of going to a funeral every weekend and seeing so many people hungry, without enough food to take with their medicine." As I continued to listen, she described herself as "an endangered married woman," forced to leave her husband because he was fooling around.

My heart was troubled by that conversation in so many ways. Her wariness about treatment possibilities reminded me that just a few weeks earlier I had been talking to the leader of people living with HIV and AIDS in Jakarta, Indonesia. I asked Anna, an incredibly positive and courageous woman fighting against waves of stigma and discrimination in a predominately Muslim country, what made her angry. She replied, "I can't stand to hear of yet another person dying because they followed the advice of a Pentecostal preacher telling them to stop taking the medicines and just pray." Prayer can be powerful medicine for the soul, but it's a cruel substitute for reliable high-quality antiretroviral drugs and good nutrition.

———

These four vignettes are reminders of how daily, in forgotten hidden corners of the world, hunger and AIDS often interact to form a deadly combination for thousands of people. Thailand, where the tragedy of Khin Myo Bu unfolded, remains one of the economic and political tigers of Southeast Asia. It has made significant progress in combating poverty and stimulating new wealth and opportunities. Paula Gill's dilemma took place in Barbados, a popular, prosperous tourist island attracting visitors from Europe and the United States. William Kahangi struggled for survival on the streets of Eldoret in Kenya, a country where one in four adults is infected with HIV and 11 percent of the children are AIDS orphans. (Kenya's infection rate was estimated at 14 percent in the mid-1990s and declined to 5 percent by 2006.) Once a shining symbol of democracy and progress on the continent of Africa, Kenya is sliding into political violence and social instability, with crime rates rising and poverty increasing. And Zoe Mbeki's future is very uncertain in a post-apartheid South Africa, a country ravaged by HIV and AIDS and the victim of public policies that have sometimes bordered on a genocide of indifference.

Hunger and the Globalization of AIDS

A Canadian, Marshall McLuhan, first popularized the vision of the world as a global village, in the 1960s. Although the idea ignored many of the sharp economic, religious, and cultural differences that characterize different parts of the globe, it emphasized the unity of humanity on a planet shrinking due to new forms of transportation and communication.

On the positive side, this image envisioned a world without borders, where people would see their diversity as a gift and their neighbors as sisters and brothers. It presented an understanding that reminds us of our interconnectedness, regardless of nationality, race, gender, sexual orientation, or religion.

On the negative side, we have discovered that the new forces of globalization often resemble the old faces of colonialism; the powerful and the rich still dominate world economies and politics. The benefits of free trade are offset by the exploitation of the poor, and the winds of westernization have little or no respect for local or regional histories or traditions.

As the world has become a global village, we have discovered that hunger has increased and diseases no longer can be quarantined to simply one region or locale. All that glitters about globalization is not gold: there is a dark, dreadful side to what happens to people and the environment under its influence.

Truly, AIDS is the first disease of globalization. This pandemic has swept the earth and has become the world's worst health crisis in seven hundred years. Global malnutrition has escalated as HIV has killed farmers, reduced economic solvency of families, and weakened national productivity. People suffering with HIV and AIDS need more food, not less. But tragically, it is abundantly evident that in today's world "the rich get health and the poor are seen as expendable."[5]

Global AIDS and World Hunger

Most conversations and books about HIV and AIDS focus almost exclusively on the fact that it is primarily a sexually transmitted disease. Overlooked, especially in the United States, is the fact that HIV and AIDS are both a cause and a consequence of poverty in today's world. Or, to put it another way, hunger is both a cause and a consequence of HIV and AIDS. While not ignoring the sexual dimension of this disease, this book's primary focus is to demonstrate the links between poverty, particularly hunger, and the HIV and AIDS pandemic.

The stigma of being HIV positive prevails around the world. One of my Asian colleagues had a brother who was dying of AIDS, but my colleague couldn't tell his academic or clerical colleagues because the family forbade him to out of embarrassment, fear of how their children would be treated, and uncertainty whether the brother's employer might dismiss him. This suffering silence even meant that the brother's wife didn't seek treatment for HIV, and thus she died quickly of AIDS. As a result, three orphans were added to the world's roster of vulnerable children, and my friend had to expand his family at great economic and personal sacrifice.

Chapter Two

The Faces of Global HIV and AIDS

Nearly thirty years into the global HIV and AIDS pandemic, and after more than nearly 65 million people have been infected, a conspiracy of silence still prevails in many places. Former United Nations secretary general Kofi Annan has repeatedly said that the first battle to contend with in the global AIDS emergency is to "break the conspiracy of silence at every level." Annan laments, "In too many countries an official conspiracy of silence about AIDS has denied people information that could have saved their lives."[1]

I saw the consequences of this silence when I visited impoverished Burma (Myanmar), where totalitarian military leaders have long denied the seriousness of AIDS within their country. Now the AIDS pandemic is exploding into the general population, and belatedly members of the junta are beginning to acknowledge it may be more widespread than they have admitted. On the outskirts of Yangon (Rangoon), I sat on the floor of a wooden shack with a group of men and women living with HIV/AIDS. As we shared bread and water, these mothers and fathers asked me to break the silence and be a voice for the voiceless of Burma.

As I bade farewell to my hospitable HIV-positive host, who was holding his five-year-old daughter and fifteen-month-old son, my broken heart pondered their future and the fate of hundreds of millions more like them throughout Asia. I kept hearing a proverb from the Hebrew Bible: "Speak up for those who cannot speak...defend the rights of the poor and needy" (Proverbs 31: 8–9).

In a small, makeshift clinical office outside a Soweto-area hospital in Johannesburg, South Africa, the silence was pierced by the penetrating wail of a mother and grandmother who had just lost their baby to AIDS. As the haunting sounds echoed in the souls of my wife and myself, we heard a psychologist describe the conspiracy of silence as a "genocide of indifference" in Sub-Saharan Africa.

I felt the silence when I visited the largest AIDS hospital in southern India, located in a village outside Chennai called Tambaram. Greeting me were more than eight hundred women, children, and men who were struggling to survive HIV and AIDS without any life-sustaining antiretroviral medicine. The evil of stigmatization and discrimination looms especially large in the women's wards. Not only were the women dying, but they were dying alone.

I listened to the silence when a young woman came to me in tears to tell me about the plight of women and children in heroin-infested northeast India. With their husbands and fathers dying from AIDS, they faced abandonment and rejection and were forced out of their homes into a camp outside the city boundaries. In order to survive, in order to buy food for themselves and their children, they engage in what many glibly call prostitution, but in reality amounts to nothing more than survival sex so they can feed their children. Nobody in the world cares for these women and children. Unless someone intervenes, soon the silence of non-caring will contribute to their suffering and death by AIDS.

Former president Nelson Mandela, the hero of South Africa, broke the conspiracy of silence when he announced that his son had died from HIV/AIDS. He invited us all to share his sorrow and to face frankly what the United Nations has called a global emergency. It is one of the greatest challenges facing this generation. Failure to act creatively and compassionately is to forsake humanity. Failure to reach out to the people with programs of education and prevention is to invite disease and death. Failure to offer care and treatment is to betray our values of championing the dignity of all life.

Nearly thirty years into the global HIV and AIDS pandemic, the challenge remains of overcoming the conspiracy of silence that too often prevails. Despite widespread death and suffering throughout the world, combating HIV and AIDS simply has not been a priority for most people.

Combating an Imminent Terrorist Threat: A Virus Called HIV

The world faces an imminent threat, and the terrorist is called HIV. Once a person is infected with HIV, the virus depletes a subset of lymphocytes called T4 helper cells, or CD4+ cells, that are crucial for cell-mediated immunity and the production of antibodies. This leaves the body vulnerable to many other diseases. AIDS appears at the end of chronic HIV infection. Technically, people do not actually die of AIDS, but from other opportunistic diseases that take advantage of a failed immune system.

This terrorist in our midst shows no favoritism; it attacks people of all races, ages, countries, genders, and sexual orientations. An attack from this terrorist, however, can be prevented, as it is not transmitted casually by touching, or sharing food, or even by ordinary kissing.

Two types of education are needed globally for the fight against HIV and AIDS to truly become a successful endeavor. First, we must educate the uninformed. Vast multitudes of people worldwide do not know what HIV is, how it is transmitted, or what needs to happen after a person is infected. Second, we must also educate the misinformed, combating misunderstanding and fear, which only contribute to increased stigmatization and discrimination and promote improper prevention methods and inadequate patient care.

Knowing how HIV is transmitted is critical. HIV is not spread by everyday, ordinary contact with a person who is infected. It is primarily transmitted through (1) sexual relationships (anal, vaginal, and oral) with an infected person, (2) exposure to infected blood (generally through a transfusion of contaminated blood or through contaminated needles shared among intravenous drug users), and (3) mother-to-infant transmission (either during pregnancy, in childbirth, or through breast-feeding).

Knowing how to prevent the transmission of HIV is also critical. People can protect themselves if they have knowledge and resources available. In the case of sexual contact, the correct and consistent use of condoms is highly effective. Condoms do not provide 100 percent effectiveness, but they are the world's best "weapon of mass protection" available. The distribution of free or low-cost quality condoms is imperative, but too often they are too expensive or unavailable to the poor in Africa, Asia, and Latin America.

The passage of HIV through needle sharing is extremely prevalent in certain regions, especially in eastern European countries and in the so-called Golden Triangle of northeast India, Burma, and Thailand. Harm-reduction programs reduce the number of HIV infections by helping to eliminate needle sharing. However, political and community leaders hesitate to support these programs because they provide clean needles and there is the fear that this will only encourage intravenous drug usage.

At this point in time there is no vaccine to prevent HIV and no cure for HIV and AIDS. It is possible, however, for people to live with the disease, but this is contingent upon lifetime access to antiretroviral drugs and proper care, including medication, nutritious food, and clean water. Though a manageable chronic disease, HIV often means living with uncomfortable side effects and frequent changes of medication. Once antiretroviral medications are begun, they dare not be withdrawn without risking severe consequences.

Medications are available to greatly reduce the risk of passage of HIV to a child during pregnancy and the birth process. Sadly, these drugs are rarely available to the women who need them most. HIV infections can also occur during breast-feeding, but without access to formula or clean water, the mothers have no choice but to breast-feed their babies.

Beyond Theological Taboos to a Theology of Life

Coping with this global scenario of HIV and AIDS challenges religious people of all faiths to reexamine their theological perspectives. At the fifteenth International AIDS Conference, held in Bangkok, Thailand, in 2004, it was evident that theological taboos have contributed to the escalating HIV/AIDS crisis. Clearly, the religious roots of this disease must be reviewed to determine how the theological thinking of some has caused widespread harm to many.

The first theological taboo has been not talking openly about sex, preventing people from understanding how to prevent the disease. Second, moralistic judgments toward infected people and their families have added to society's stigmatization. Third, religious prejudice toward sex workers, intravenous-drug users, men who have sex with men, and others have contributed to discrimination. Silence, stigma, and discrimination keep people from getting tested and treated. Most people with HIV and AIDS say that worse than the disease is the way people treat them and their families.

An AIDS theology focused only on personal sin

is inadequate to deal with the complexity of those sinned against: people imprisoned by poverty, discrimination, racism, and cultural/societal structures over which they have no control. Patriarchal religious assumptions have made women especially vulnerable. In many countries, married women and young girls are endangered because they lack education and control of their own sex lives. Endless controversies over the efficacy of condoms have helped deny people the least expensive weapon of mass protection available.

The vicious sins of stigmatization and discrimination must be identified and resisted, and every person's worth and dignity respected. Religious people, be they Christians, Muslims, Jews, Buddhists, or Hindus, can combat stigmatization and discrimination in society and their faith communities by offering love, acceptance, forgiveness, and healing, not judgment and prejudice. It does not cost any money to proclaim that stigmatizing and discriminating are sins against the will of God.

Some religious communities around the world have done pioneering work in the battle against HIV and AIDS, but often their good deeds have been obscured by the publicity given to a twisted theology claiming that AIDS is the punishment of God. This has prompted people to embrace a theology of condemnation rather than compassion, indifference rather than involvement, and labeling rather than liberation. Instead of offering a theology of hope and health, faith-based groups sometimes have become missionaries of death, not life.

Twin Killers: Stigma and Silence

A theological student in India was diagnosed with HIV. Later that same day the faculty of his seminary convened and voted to discharge him from his ministerial studies. The next day the young man committed suicide.

This tragic event symbolizes how stigma kills and how it contributes to a deadly culture of silence that fuels the HIV and AIDS pandemic. If religious and educational institutions fail to show compassion and care for people living with HIV and AIDS, then it is inevitable that the death count from AIDS will continue to climb in Asia, Africa, and elsewhere in the world.

This incident dramatizes the need for asking questions. What if the young man had known how to protect himself from the virus? What if he had been provided counseling about how he could live a good, and possibly long, life using antiretroviral medicines? What if faculty had reached out to him with understanding and loving arms, helping him see the possibilities for Christian ministry to others, especially others living with HIV and AIDS? What if his theological college had not been so judgmental, instead showing Christ-like compassion and care? What if he had lived among people who encouraged programs of education and prevention? What if the sins of stigmatization and discrimination had not been so dominate in the theology and the spirit of his church?

A friend recently wrote to me that the culture of

silence in northeast India is dangerously contributing to genocide:

> [My] brother died of AIDS earlier than
> expected because of the virus of silence and
> his wife will follow him shortly. The culture of
> silence is very strong in this part of the world.
> I used to speak of the danger of silence, but
> when my own family got affected, I, too, was
> also reluctant to speak about it openly. Imag-
> ine, after speaking so many times about the
> danger of silence, if I am finding it difficult to
> speak out, what will others do?
>
> I realize that there is a great need to edu-
> cate people to break the culture of silence. AIDS
> is spreading very fast in India, and many fami-
> lies are seriously affected. Many families are
> crying silently; pastors seldom touch on health
> issues in their preaching ministry. NGOs
> [nongovernmental organizations] working
> among rural villages tell me that the culture
> of silence is a serious matter. Several counsel-
> ors report the greatest danger is silence. Some
> persons refuse to take medicine or go to the
> hospital because of the stigma associated with
> AIDS. They fear that other people will come to
> know and stop visiting them.

Despite the fact that today 33.4 million people
are infected with HIV, and over 25 million people
have already died, a culture and conspiracy of silence

still prevails in many places. This silence fuels the pandemic by helping to create stigma, and it prohibits people from learning how to protect themselves from this vicious virus. People are afraid to get tested because of the way others in their families, neighborhoods, workplaces, and faith communities may react. Also, people often pretend that the trade in dangerous intravenous drugs so rampant in many regions of the world is not impacting those within their own families and communities. And people are especially afraid to talk candidly about human sexuality. So instead of getting tested, they pretend they are healthy, and as a result end up infecting beloved wives or partners with HIV.

Denial combined with stigma and silence inhibits people from openly advocating policies of prevention and care, and thus contributes significantly to the spread of the pandemic.

A Global Pandemic More Future Than Past

We must realize that we are only at the beginning of this pandemic. When we outline the global scenario of HIV and AIDS, we are looking more into the future than the past. Unless dramatic and systematic efforts are undertaken globally, some health experts fear this pandemic might not peak until 2040. Regardless of when it peaks, humanity will be experiencing a holocaust of unspeakable suffering and loss of life.

UNAIDS reported that in 2004, about 5 million people became infected with HIV, more than in any previous year in history. At least 2 million people lose their lives to the disease annually, though no one will ever know the exact numbers since stigmatization and inadequate health systems distort actual causes of death. Due to inadequate global tracking and health infrastructures, plus a lack of honesty in government reporting, nobody actually knows the precise numbers. As of the end of 2009, UNAIDS estimates the following range of infection statistics:[2]

Area	Range	
	Low	*High*
North America	1,200,000	1,600,000
Western Europe	710,000	970,000
Eastern Europe and Central Asia	1,400,000	1,700,000
Caribbean	220,000	260,000
North Africa and Middle East	250,000	380,000
East Asia	700,000	1,000,000
South and Southeast Asia	3,400,000	4,300,000
Latin America	1,800,000	2,200,000
Sub-Saharan Africa	20,800,000	24,100,000
Oceania	51,000	68,000

Speaking in figures of thousands and millions of people sometimes blurs the reality of the disease. We are talking about people who are struggling to survive, mothers and fathers trying to provide for their families, children trying to cope with a mysterious disease that kills their beloved family members and friends, young men and women in the prime of life facing an incurable sickness. What do statistics of this nature mean? Translated into human terms, they mean that:

- A grandmother near Durban, South Africa, struggles to find enough food and energy to care for her six grandchildren, all orphaned due to HIV/AIDS. Now she is faced with an additional dilemma. Should she accept two more orphaned children who have nowhere else to go?
- A young man in Chennai, in southern India, faces an impossible decision. He has enough money on a regular basis to purchase life-sustaining antiretroviral AIDS drugs for one person. But both his parents need them. Should he buy them for his father or his mother?
- A college student in Rangoon, Burma (Myanmar), needs tuition money plus funds to support her impoverished parents and siblings. With no other possibility of employment in a totalitarian state, should she risk catching HIV by selling her body while engaging in survival sex?
- A community health leader in rural Kenya struggles to care for 1,300 vulnerable AIDS orphans. Florence knows orphanages of that size are not only unsustainably expensive, but are often emotionally detrimental to children. But how can she find money for nutrition, school uniforms, and extra expenses so elderly relatives and neighbors can provide safe guardianship and care?

Never forget the heartbreak and hopelessness, fear and anxiety, pain and suffering that confront people everywhere.

Tracking Five Trends in the Global Pandemic

Several trends need to be identified in this global scenario. *First, almost half of the infected people worldwide are women.* In Sub-Saharan Africa women make up about 61 percent of people with HIV and AIDS. Women are physically and culturally more vulnerable to the disease. Patriarchal cultures and religions contribute to the spread of the disease, as women have less autonomy and freedom to protect themselves.

The "feminization" of AIDS is evident as every year brings an increase in the percentage of women infected with HIV. Due to gender inequality, women suffer even greater stigma and discrimination in many countries. Because of the sexual behavior of men, married women may be the most endangered species on earth.

Second, the pandemic is affecting young people in disproportionate numbers. Half of all newly HIV-infected people worldwide are between the ages of fifteen and twenty-four. More than 1,150 young people contract the virus every day (an estimated 420,000 annually, down from 460,000 in 2001).

We live in a world where nearly half of the globe's population is less than twenty-five years old. Since teenagers and young adults are typically among the most sexually active and most exposed to the possibility of using intravenous drugs, HIV poses a particular threat. Young people are exposed to the disease in different ways in different areas. For example, in Sub-Saharan Africa the main mode of transmission is through heterosexual intercourse, while in eastern Europe and central Asia HIV prevalence among young people is escalating due primarily to injecting drugs with contaminated equipment and unsafe sex. Young gay men in all cultures are especially vulnerable. In many cultures and countries the term *gay* is rejected or denied, but the reality persists that men worldwide have sex with other men. Because homosexuality has been criminalized in many countries in Africa as well as in countries such as India, prevention messages are often not targeted to this significant population.

A third trend is the growing number of children orphaned due to HIV/AIDS. From 2001 to 2008 the number of AIDS-related orphans increased from 11.5 million to 15 million. The United Nations Children's Fund projects there could be as many as 50 million orphans in Sub-Saharan Africa in the next few years. Every fourteen seconds an African child loses a parent to AIDS. Likewise in Asia, the numbers of orphans and other vulnerable children is increasing.

Of course the best way to help children is to advocate for care and treatment that will keep their parents alive. The scandal of the world is that the rich get medicine, but not the poor. Over 90 percent of the people infected in economically developing countries do not get antiretroviral drugs. The World Health Organization reports that fewer than 16 percent of

HIV-positive people in the Asia-Pacific region who need antiretroviral drugs are actually receiving them.

If keeping the parents alive is not possible, finding means to nurture the children in caring, loving ways in the extended family is desirable. Unfortunately, too often the orphans themselves are stigmatized by their parents' disease and are treated with prejudice, even among their extended families. Establishing group homes and orphanages is also essential, though more desirable is creating programs and networks that keep children safely in their own communities rather than risking alienating them further by placing them in institutions. Creating community-based care systems and/or orphanages requires great commitment and loving service. Because some orphans themselves are infected with HIV/AIDS, care and treatment must be part of the plan. Tragically, today's orphanages must include hospices to care for dying children.

A fourth trend emphasizes that AIDS increasingly has an Asian face. No longer can the pandemic solely be identified with the West or Africa. One-quarter of the 3 million new infections in 2003 were in Asia. In the early years of the twenty-first century, it appears that the epicenter of the epidemic, as measured in sheer numbers, has been shifting to Asia, home to more than half of the world's population. A small increase in infection rates can impact millions and millions of people.

Yet statistics emerging from Asia are unclear and often confusing. An earlier, widely distributed

assessment from the National Intelligence Council predicted that by 2010 China would have 10 to
15 million HIV/AIDS cases, India 20 to 25 million,
Russia 5 to 8 million, Nigeria 10 to 15 million, and
Ethiopia 7 to 10 million.[3] These projections appear to
be outdated or incorrect as UNAIDS has refined its
methods of estimating deaths and infections. Since
many governments either lack accurate information
or are secretive about data and conditions in their
countries, mathematical projections remain problematic. Recent statistical studies and successful prevention efforts have reduced the forecasts, particularly as India and China appear to be taking more
assertive action at prevention after years of denial.

The World Bank forecasts that if urgent steps
are not taken to prevent the spread of HIV, the number of new HIV infections in India could increase to
5.5 million annually by 2033 and be the leading cause
of death in the country. Some believe that the disease
already has spread beyond high-risk groups into the
general population. In contrast, the Indian government asserts that the increase in number of new HIV
cases is stabilizing and that the country will not rep-
licate the prevalence rates of Sub-Saharan Africa.[4]

India's HIV and AIDS statistics have long
proved difficult to determine. At one point, UNAIDS
declared that India had more HIV cases than any
other country in the world. Later this was revised
substantially, dropping from an estimated 5.1 million HIV and AIDS cases to 2.5 million. South
Africa is once again deemed the nation with the

largest number of infections and the highest number of new infections per day. Grassroots AIDS activists in India believe their country's number is larger than currently reported, but there is no proven method to determine the reality. The acknowledged number of cases in India fails to account for the HIV-positive people in the country who are unaware of their HIV status or have not been reported for another reason.

India's government slowly has begun to face this new reality. Richard Feachem, executive director of the Global Fund to Fight AIDS, Tuberculosis, and Malaria, warned that the Indian HIV/AIDS pandemic was "on an African trajectory...and incidence of HIV/AIDS is rising rapidly."[5] Bill Gates of the Gates Foundation says that "the choice is now clear and stark: India can either be the home of the world's largest and most devastating AIDS epidemic—or, with the support of the rest of the world, it can become the best example of how this virus can be defeated."[6]

The fifth trend to be noted is how HIV and AIDS are increasing in the United States, especially in the African American community. Every nine and a half minutes, an American is infected.

HIV and AIDS touch every corner of the earth. In the United States, 1.4 million people are estimated to be infected, but one-fourth of those do not know it. So, potentially every day those infected with HIV risk infecting someone else. This phenomenon is replicated around the world. Due to the fear of being diagnosed HIV positive and the lack of available, inexpensive, confidential ways of being tested, the virus continues to spread unimpeded.

In the United States half of all new infections occur in the African American community. Due to a variety of factors including homophobia, mistrust of the medical community, incarceration rates, racism, poverty, and lack of HIV education, testing and treatment often comes far too late. HIV and AIDS have not yet exploded into the general populations of many countries, but for the purpose of better understanding the crisis confronting humanity, let us look particularly at the continents of Africa and Asia.

The African Face of AIDS

In the mid-1990s, antiretroviral medicines became available in the more affluent countries of the world. The pills were not a cure, but they finally ended what was a horrifying nightmare of people infected with HIV dying daily in the United States and Europe as medical professionals struggled without any effective medicine. As death rates dropped dramatically, a gigantic sigh of relief swept through US and western European societies and an apathetic sleep descended upon their public authorities. Simultaneously, southern Africa was experiencing a perfect storm of hunger, poverty, violence, gender inequality, and a rampaging virus called HIV.

In the movie *A Closer Walk*, a dramatic scene shows the Clinton administration bringing a young woman from Uganda to speak at the White House about her HIV infection and what was happening in her country. She spoke before a rapt audience including Vice President Al Gore. But to the dismay of film viewers, the young woman is sent back to Uganda to die, without a supply of antiretroviral drugs. She had a name and a face, but she became just another number and fact to the US administration and public.

Today, African nations, particularly those south of the Sahara, are the most impacted by the pandemic. Africans make up 70 percent of the adults and 80 percent of the children who are infected in the world. Three-quarters of all the people who have died since the beginning of the pandemic came from this region of the world. South Africa remains the country with the most people infected in the world: more than 5 million.

Women are the primary face of HIV and AIDS in Africa. Some 60 percent of those infected are women. Unlike in the United States, where initially HIV and AIDS were associated primarily with somewhat affluent, white, gay males, the African portrait is of poor, black, heterosexual females. War, poverty, drought, malnutrition, migration, unemployment, limited healthcare, lack of education, and other infectious diseases all contributed to the rapid spread of HIV and AIDS into almost every village, attacking the most vulnerable of the world.

What especially marked the spread of AIDS in Africa was that most infections were triggered by heterosexual relationships. Culturally, a widespread acceptance of multiple sexual partners enabled the virus to spread beyond commercial sex workers into the general population. The commonplace situation of married men having more than one sexual partner simultaneously prompted one African woman to say, "I used to fear for my unmarried daughters, but now my greatest fear is for my married daughters." Women who are denied civil and legal rights find themselves unable to have control over their own bodies or to resist the sexual demands of men. Cultural practices such as "cleansing," which requires a woman newly widowed to have sexual intercourse with her husband's older brother or some professional sex "cleanser," have aided and abetted the spread in certain tribal areas.

These and other factors in Africa have all contributed to wide-scale suffering and death, causing the life expectancy rate to drop in many countries and impacting economic development, particularly in terms of agricultural production. As farmers have died, hunger has increased, and knowledge about the art of farming has not been passed on to future generations. Grandparents and the elderly have been forced to return to heavy farm labor and to raise children at a time in life when their energies and health are depleted. Poverty has escalated while health services have deteriorated, social welfare has diminished, and public education has declined.

The Asian Face of AIDS

In a report called *AIDS in Asia: Face the Facts*, it is noted that what propels the increase of HIV/AIDS in Asia is somewhat different than in Africa and some other parts of the world.[7] Note five factors that fuel the Asian pandemic.

First, *"in Asia, more people engage in commercial sex than in any other behavior that carries a high risk of HIV infection."* It is estimated that more than half of all infections have been contracted during commercial sex. No one knows the proportion of men who buy sex, but the practice is more widespread than generally acknowledged.

Second, *the explosive growth of HIV among intravenous drug users (IDUs) is increasing the Asian pandemic.* Very few countries have reliable estimates of the number of people who inject drugs, but it is known that there is widespread needle and syringe sharing in Asia. Sections of China, India, Myanmar, Thailand, and Vietnam have all recorded very high levels of HIV infection among IDUs.

Third, *Asian countries generally underreport the prevalence of men who have sex with men and tend to ignore this behavior in prevention programs.* Since homosexual sex is ignored, safer sex practices often do not prevail, thus homosexual sex has become one of the main engines of growth of the pandemic in Asia.

Fourth, there is *"a kaleidoscope of risk,"* since *the above behaviors interact.* Various combinations promote the spread of HIV into other parts of the population. Someone who got the disease as an IDU can give it to a sex worker or his partner. Men who have commercial sex may later have sex with their wives or other women. Men who have sex with men often also may have sex with women.

Fifth, other factors also spread the disease in Asia. These include unsafe medical practices in hospitals and clinics, inadequate supervision of the blood supply, lonely truck drivers who are away from their homes for months at a time, the migration of people for employment (especially men) to and from rural areas, and the failure of governments to demonstrate leadership and provide sufficient healthcare funding.

Promoting the Alphabet of Life

Young people hold the hope for the future, since their actions will shape the future of the pandemic. In the few countries of the world that have successfully decreased HIV infection, it is because their youth have been provided honest, open, and frank information, and the young have made safer behavioral choices. If governments and nongovernmental organizations are to be lifesaving and life-giving institutions, then they must openly address sex education and the use of intravenous drugs in ways that reflect the best insights of science and public health, without falling into the old traps of moralistic judgment, shame, and stigmatization, which only alienate youth rather than liberate them from the dangers of HIV and AIDS.

Remember, hope exists. Unlike with many diseases, such as cancer, sickle-cell anemia, or multiple sclerosis, medical scientists know how to keep people from contracting HIV. Comprehensive prevention programs can reduce the possibilities of infection. Because the global AIDS pandemic involves talking about sexuality, intravenous drug use, condom distribution, lubrication, prostitution, men who have sex with men, and so on, the issues addressed are not always easy, pretty, or simple; in fact, they are rather difficult and sometimes embarrassing. Yet people are suffering and dying at astronomical rates, and these life and death issues must be addressed.

Emphasizing the ABCs of prevention requires teaching about abstinence, being faithful to one's partner, and correctly and consistently using condoms. A world without AIDS, however, requires more than the ABCs of prevention. Abstinence, faithfulness, and condoms are not enough to rid the globe of the scourge of HIV and AIDS. Attention must also focus on the structural dimensions of society, culture, and religion that aid and abet the spread of this disease. Leadership eager to end AIDS must go beyond the personal questions and face the political issues that underlie this global catastrophe.

The alphabet of life requires focusing on the *D* of AIDS prevention: namely, economic and social development as envisioned by the Millennium Development Goals that were outlined in the first chapter. Poverty in all its forms must be confronted and alleviated if the HIV and AIDS pandemics are to subside. An overwhelming percentage of people infected in the world live below poverty line, whether they live in South Africa, South Dakota, or Southeast Asia. The letter *D* could also be a reference to illustrate the need for destroying dirty needles used in intravenous injections of usually illegal drugs and ensuring access to clean needles.

E stands for promoting gender equality. For many women and girls in this world, the ABC approach is insufficient because women and children lack the social and economic power to have appropriate autonomy over their own lives, and they often live in fear of male violence. Many women labeled as prostitutes or sex workers are actually forced into survival sex for money in order to live and care for their families. As the Salvation Army leader told some of us when we visited the vast red-light district of Mumbai, we should think of these women as our sisters, for we are all a part of the human family. Only as the role and status of women in the world is elevated will the spread of HIV and AIDS begin to recede.

And finally, *F* needs to be emphasized, representing the essential nutritional food that hungry people around the world must obtain on a consistent basis. When visiting a food kitchen in Denver, I was reminded by a volunteer that "desperate people do desperate things when they need food for their families and themselves." In a world of 1.2 billion hungry people, the possibilities for risky behavior to obtain food are widespread. Whether it is a matter of trading sexual favors or stealing, people struggling to exist tomorrow will not worry about the long-term effects of a virus they cannot see or a crime they hope to escape today.

Belatedly, almost thirty years into the pandemic, people of all walks of life, along with their leaders, finally must demonstrate a new willingness to participate in positive partnerships with governments and nongovernmental organizations engaged in programs of education, prevention, care, and treatment. For every person *infected*, at least another ten family members are *affected*. Multiply 33.4 million people by ten, and you can feel the ocean waves of tears flooding the earth. When will a new rainbow of hope, health, and help emerge in the midst of this global tsunami?

As the global recession escalated in 2009, parents in Kenya were often unable to feed their young children. Hearing that a little church in the horrid Kibera slums of Nairobi sometimes had food, in desperation they simply abandoned their loved little ones in the sanctuary in hopes that they would be fed.

chapter Three

World Hunger: Cause and Consequence of Global AIDS

When Peter Piot, the former head of UNAIDS, visited Malawi, he met with a group of women living with HIV and AIDS. In the course of the conversation, he quizzed them as to what was their highest priority. "Their answer was clear and unanimous. Not care. Not drugs for treatment. Not relief from stigma. But food."[1]

But the world has not heard or heeded the women of Malawi. "Access for All" was the headline theme of the fifteenth International AIDS Conference, held in Bangkok, Thailand, in 2004. Attention primarily focused on the urgent moral and medical necessity of providing access to antiretroviral therapies to every person on earth in need. However, at that international gathering and during subsequent conferences focused on global AIDS, insufficient attention was given to the corollary need to promise and provide access for all to the world's plentiful food supply. For without food security and proper nutrition, the dream of renewed health attributable to antiretroviral therapy proves to be an illusion. One AIDS activist in India told me that in some parts of his country people are being killed by the drugs because of inadequate food and nutrition. Perhaps that is overstated, but clearly, inadequate attention has been given worldwide to the relationship of medicine and food in treating HIV and AIDS.

World food production has suffered setbacks due to the deaths of millions of farmers from AIDS. Because this disease often strikes at the most productive citizens, those who are in their twenties and thirties, there is no one to farm except weary and often frail grandparents and young children. Bread for the World reports that one in three people south of the Sahara desert suffer from hunger. Seeds cannot be planted or crops harvested if the farmers are too sick. Hungry AIDS orphans and their grandparents reportedly even dig up roots for food. World hunger is both a cause and consequence of global HIV and AIDS.

Major International Efforts at Providing Treatment

As a follow-up to the adoption of the Millennium Development Goals, the United Nations met in a special session in 2001 for its first-ever public health debate. One hundred eighty-nine countries signed the Declaration of Commitment on HIV and AIDS that resulted from these deliberations. They deemed the global AIDS crisis a global emergency and set a series of targets to meet by the end of 2005. These included:

- Reduce HIV prevalence by 25 percent among persons aged fifteen to twenty-four;
- Ensure that 90 percent of young people have access to education and services;
- Reduce infant infection by 20 percent;
- Increase annual spending to $7 to $10 billion.

When the UN returned to evaluate progress five years later, in 2006, they acknowledged failure in achieving these and other efforts, but they reaffirmed their commitment and underscored the need for addressing the crisis.

Of critical importance was the establishment of the Global Fund to Fight AIDS, Tuberculosis, and Malaria in 2001. By 2009, it had approved grants worth $11.3 billion addressing these three diseases across 137 countries.

The Global Fund to date has provided antiretroviral treatment for 2.3 million people with HIV, DOTS (directly observed treatment short course) for 5.4 million patients with tuberculosis, and 74 million treatments for people with malaria (plus 88 million insecticide-treated bed nets). A report issued in 2007 indicated that 3,000 lives were being saved daily by the fund, another 1.5 million cases of AIDS and tuberculosis had been prevented, plus 33 million malaria episodes had been avoided. The 770,000 people now with access to antiretroviral therapy thanks to the Global Fund are estimated to live a total of 290,000 additional years.[2] The Global Fund currently "supports more than 30 percent of HIV/AIDS programs, about two-thirds of the tuberculosis treatments, and 45 percent of malaria treatment programs worldwide."[3] Precarious funding persistently plagues this effort, as nations are quicker to make pledges than to actually pay for these international efforts.

In December 2003, the World Health Organization (WHO) launched the 3 by 5 Initiative. An ambitious plan, the goal was to provide antiretroviral treatment to 3 million people by the end of 2005. Never before had WHO taken such an aggressive stance on addressing a public health issue, and it soon discovered it lacked the capacity to deliver on the promises it made. Near the end of 2005, then-director Dr. Lee Jong-wook publicly apologized for failing to achieve this vision, even though remarkable progress had been made and about 1.6 million people were under treatment at that time. These efforts continue.

The 3 by 5 Initiative was a learning experience for WHO and the global community. The actual initiative ended in December 2005; however, even now we are learning and taking cues from these great efforts to stop the pandemic. While the initiative did not reach its goal of 3 million people, it is believed that in the two years of the initiative, between 250,000 and 350,000 deaths were prevented.[4]

As with many of the programs put in place to help with the pandemic, the 3 by 5 Initiative did not realize the fundamental lack of an infrastructure to help provide the widespread care needed for the antiretrovirals to be dispersed. When trying to combat AIDS, there is much more at stake than just getting the medications needed to the people who need them. Hunger, gender inequality, and poverty are all closely related to the spread of the AIDS epidemic. Without a well-organized and comprehensive plan on how to create an infrastructure that penetrates all of these issues, one program cannot provide for most people. But due to the 3 by 5 Initiative, a process began that will help future work to provide for the countries hit the hardest by the disease. The initiative has taken steps to build the needed "infrastructure, including [building] clinics, laboratories, and [providing] training for health-care workers."[5]

In 2004, President George W. Bush startled the nation during his State of the Union address when he announced unexpectedly that he was asking for $15 billion to address the HIV and AIDS crisis, the largest expenditure of funds ever envisioned for a single disease. Bush underscored the mounting disaster in Africa and the Caribbean by launching the President's Emergency Plan for AIDS Relief (PEPFAR).

Despite controversy over details of the effort (namely, how much funding should be directed toward abstinence programs versus toward funding for promoting condom usage), President Bush's plan met with strong bipartisan support. Critics complained that the effort reflected America's go-it-alone approach to foreign affairs and that the amount invested was proportionally lower to start than other countries have contributed. However, no one disputes the fact that the United States has invested far more overall than any other nation. No country comes close to matching what the United States has invested in programs like PEPFAR, the Global Fund, and the US Agency for International Development.

PEPFAR is making slow progress on its promised goals, but it is making progress nonetheless. The initial goal was to give $15 billion over a five-year period to improve the HIV and AIDS services in some of the areas most severely affected. With this money, the plan was to (1) treat 2 million people infected with HIV; (2) help prevent 7 million new HIV infections; and (3) care for 10 million people infected and affected by HIV and AIDS.[6] At this time PEPFAR has provided antiretroviral treatment to more than 1 million men, women, and children throughout Sub-Saharan Africa, Asia, and the Caribbean; 52,000 people have been trained in providing quality care to people with HIV and AIDS; and the plan has supported community outreach activities to nearly 61.5 million people to prevent the sexual transmission of the virus.[7] With continued efforts and open dialogue about the many issues supporting the spread of HIV and AIDS, the PEPFAR program hopes to meet and exceed its goals.

The most enduring positive legacy of President Bush will likely be his initiatives to address HIV and AIDS, particularly in Africa. In his final State of the Union address, on February 28, 2008, the president asked for a five-year, $30 billion extension of PEPFAR. He envisioned increasing the number of people receiving access to antiretroviral drugs through PEPFAR from 1.4 million to 2.5 million, as well as providing prevention measures to about 12 million people.[8] Speaking to Congress for the last time as president, Bush also addressed hunger, claiming:

> America is leading the fight against global hunger. Today, more than half the world's food aid comes from the United States. And tonight, I

ask the Congress to support an innovative proposal to provide food assistance by purchasing crops directly from farmers in the developing world, so we can build up local agriculture and help break the cycle of famine.[9]

Critics argued that the $30 billion was insufficient for HIV and AIDS global efforts and did not really reflect an increase in the US level of commitment. On July 30, 2008, Bush signed new legislation authorizing up to $48 billion over the next five years to combat global HIV/AIDS, tuberculosis, and malaria. David Beckmann, president of the nonpartisan advocacy organization Bread for the World, commended Bush, saying:

What the President said about global poverty was right on the mark…The President's HIV/AIDS Initiative has shown amazing success in a very short time. However, in many regions of the world, HIV/AIDS is a disease of poverty and cannot be solved by drugs alone…Nutrition, clean water, and livelihood assistance will help achieve success in the fight against HIV/AIDS and ensure that countries can build the capacity to take on the care of their citizens in the future. Programs like the Millennium Challenge Account seek to build this sustainable capacity and deserve equal investment.

Feeding hungry people must be the number-one priority of our food aid programs.

It is scandalous that half of every food aid dollar does not go to feed those in greatest need, but into the pockets of US companies for processing, packaging, and transport. Bread for the World supports a shift from our current system to one where local purchase of emergency food aid in appropriate circumstances can be accomplished. We are pleased that President Bush used his pulpit to push for this change.[10]

Critical bipartisan legislation pending in Congress includes the Global Food Security Act of 2009. This calls for the creation of a comprehensive food security strategy, a White House coordinator to develop and oversee the strategy, and authorizes agricultural development measures critical to addressing long-term hunger around the world. Also awaiting action is the bipartisan Foreign Assistance Reform Act of 2009, which is aimed at improving US foreign assistance programs that are currently fragmented across twelve departments, twenty-five different agencies, and about sixty government offices. It requires President Barack Obama to develop and implement a comprehensive National Strategy for Global Development. President Obama is on record supporting new efforts to address both global AIDS and world hunger, but the legislative and administrative action has been delayed due to the global economic crisis, two wars, and other high-priority legislative initiatives. In the meantime, the number of hungry people in the world continues to escalate.

When the G8 leaders met in L'Aquila, Italy, in 2009, President Obama spoke of how his father grew up herding goats as a child in a Kenyan village. He noted that millions of people are facing hunger daily in villages like this around the world. Afterward, pledges from the various nations jumped from $15 billion to $20 billion.[11] Whether those pledges will ever be fully paid remains problematic, but the United States, with the largest pledge, at $3.5 billion, is pressing other nations to comply. Secretary of State Hillary Clinton declared on World Food Day 2009, "Fighting hunger and poverty through sustainable agricultural development, making sure that enough food is available and that people have resources to purchase it, is a key foreign policy objective of the Obama administration."[12]

Global AIDS and World Hunger Are Inextricably Related

Medicine alone is not enough; a consistent supply of nutritious food is imperative as a critical ingredient of an effective care and treatment program for people living with HIV and AIDS. Likewise, good nutrition is no substitute for life-extending drug therapies. Healthy foods, diets, vitamins, and so on are insufficient by themselves to protect infected people from the debilitating progress of HIV. Globally, people in need must have access to both affordable (or free) food and medicine if we are to effectively fight this escalating pandemic and move toward both an AIDS-free and hunger-free world.

Global AIDS and world hunger are inextricably related. It is no coincidence that if we sketched on a map the areas of the world with the highest incidences of HIV and AIDS, we would note that those same areas had the highest levels of malnourishment and food insecurity. Of the more than 1 billion people whom the United Nations estimates are chronically undernourished, a disproportionate percentage live in Sub-Saharan Africa, with 33 percent, and southern Asia, with 22 percent. India has more cases of HIV than any other country in Asia, and the National Family Health Survey, India estimates that half of all of India's children are malnourished. Tragically, some 43 percent of all Indian women have never heard about HIV, though India now leads in infections in Asia.

Ten Relationships between Hunger and Health

Numerous relationships exist between malnourishment and medicine, hunger and health. Ten overlapping relationships can be briefly cited.

First, hungry people cannot tolerate powerful antiretroviral medicines; empty stomachs contribute to side effects and discourage people from adhering to treatment requirements. It is strongly recommended that most of the medicine prescribed in the developed world be taken with food, yet somehow the assumption has been made that AIDS medicines can be distributed to people in these impoverished countries without regard to the nutritional needs of the patient.

Second, hungry people lack finances to buy food, much less medicine, clean water, condoms, or sanitary supplies. People who are barely making it on less than $1 a day have no resources to fall back on when illness strikes. Catherine Bertini, former head of the World Food Programme, underscores the vicious circle of poverty when she notes, "People are hungry because they are poor, and they are poor because they are hungry." Additionally, personal and family incomes decline when breadwinners are ill. Some studies suggest that when a male in a family dies from AIDS, the family's food supply can drop by as much as 70 percent.

Third, nutritious food, along with safe water, can assist people in staying healthier longer and enjoying a better quality of life. Considerable scientific literature affirms that a balanced, nutritious diet protects immune systems and makes people generally less susceptible to infections. Polluted water inevitably encourages illness, weakening the immune system and making people more prone to HIV and other infections. Sadly, nutritional diets may be sacrificed to supply other needs. For example, the high costs of traditional funerals in Africa often mean that livestock are sold to pay for coffins and other expenditures, thereby reducing availability of certain nutritional foods.

Fourth, once hungry people have weakened immune systems, they are more susceptible to infectious diseases. Malnutrition facilitates faster progress of HIV to full-blown AIDS. Remember, scientifically AIDS is not a single disease, but an immunodeficiency syndrome. Malnourished people newly infected with HIV may rapidly suffer a variety of severe diseases historically associated with AIDS, including persistent pneumonia, brain and eye infections, skin cancers, dramatic weight loss, and thrush. As biologist Gerald J. Stine observes, "New drugs now thwart these infections in modernized nations, but the vast majority of people across the world with HIV/AIDS continue to suffer these awful physical conditions."[13]

Fifth, if appropriate nutrition accompanies medication, drugs are more effective and fewer side effects occur. The efficacy of antiretroviral medicines is enhanced when a patient is getting an enriched diet at the same time. The problem is that the impoverished people of the world live on a very limited diet. In Rwanda, for example, 38 percent of the children under five are underweight, and many children reach adulthood never having tasted or even seen milk.[14] Somehow they are able to survive, though many never grow to their full potential. Former US senator and current UN Ambassador on World Hunger George S. McGovern sometimes asks his audiences "to try a little 'gruel' or a crust of bread for thirty days, and then let me know if you don't think hunger is the greatest problem in the world."

Sixth, HIV-positive people have higher than normal nutritional requirements. HIV-positive people need 50 percent more protein and up to 15 percent more calories than they regularly eat. Protein, however, is a luxury of the West, not easily obtainable by the poor of the world. Getting more and better food proves essentially impossible for most people struggling for survival with little income and limited energy, if any, to work. Furthermore, HIV-positive people may lose their appetite and even experience severe weight loss. This further weakens the immune system, leaving the person more vulnerable to a host of diseases.

Seventh, sick people may be unable to prepare nutritious food for themselves and their families. Women around the world still tend to be the preparers of food. African women are also the producers of the food, since nine of ten farmers in Africa are women. If women are unable to work, they lack financial resources to purchase needed food, and they often have no one to cook for them.

Furthermore, stigma and discrimination may lead to HIV-positive people being cast out of their homes or communities and/or lose employment, further diminishing their ability to maintain food security. For example, a young couple in Burma (Myanmar) told me that once customers learned the couple was HIV positive, they quit buying food at their little soup shop. Forced to close, they had no income to buy food for themselves and their two little children.

Eighth, good food, vitamins, and micronutrients help ward off infections, hasten recovery between bouts of illness, and can strengthen the immune system. People who have higher incomes benefit from having had financial resources, and often education about nutrition, sufficient for not only purchasing nutritious food, but also for special vitamins and micronutrients.

Heifer International urges people to fight AIDS by purchasing a cow that will be given to a deserving person in a developing country. In a fund-raising pamphlet, Heifer International makes the case that:

> Just one cow can mean the difference between a decline into severe malnutrition and a life of hope for a person living with HIV/AIDS. One cow can provide four gallons of milk a day. Each cup of milk contains protein, fat, and vitamins and minerals essential to the function of the immune system, helping those living with HIV to stave off infection for other opportunistic diseases. The high-quality protein also insures that antiretrovirals will be most effective. Any excess milk can be sold to raise money to defray the cost of drugs and treatment.[15]

Ninth, malnourished, HIV-positive pregnant women or nursing mothers increase the risk of transmission to their babies. Infected mothers are often malnourished and unable to adequately nourish their children. Nutritional supplements can help pregnant women who are HIV positive improve birth outcomes and child growth.

HIV threatens the positive values of breast-feeding, and mothers generally are encouraged not to continue breast-feeding beyond six months. However, there is no easy solution to this dilemma, since formula is expensive and safe, clean water is often unavailable.

Tenth, hungry people are more vulnerable to engaging in risky human behavior. With no other avenue to food for themselves or their family, women are often forced to engage in survival sex, selling their bodies to attain desperately needed nutrition. Young boys likewise may engage in commercial sex work in order to feed themselves and their families. In Sri Lanka, impoverished children are most vulnerable to hunger, resulting in an estimated 30,000 child sex workers.

In Haiti, a twelve-year-old child involved in commercial sex work was asked whether she knew she could get AIDS. She answered, "I am afraid. But even if I get AIDS, I'll live a few years, won't I? You see, my family has no food for tomorrow."[16] Faced with no other alternatives to starvation, how many of us would do differently?

Addressing this interrelationship between world hunger and global AIDS has to be underscored in the coming years. The vast discrepancies between the rich and the poor of our world become glaringly evident when confronting hunger and disease. Beyond analysis or paralysis, the world community has both an obligation and an opportunity to focus on both issues simultaneously.

Mahatma Gandhi once said that "to a hungry person, God can appear only as a piece of bread." In the contemporary world, he might revise his insights and say, "To a hungry person, God can appear only as a piece of bread and antiretroviral medicine." In the next chapter, we will explore how this can happen.

When I was walking through the same hospital in Eldoret, I saw a dead woman in one of the beds. I was told that hospital officials in the ward were waiting for someone else to die, and then they would place them both on the same cart and wheel them to the hospital crematorium. I remember Dr. Mamlin shaking his fist in the air and saying, "I'm going to put that place out of business!" His goal was to stop the endless dying and get proper food and antiretroviral medicine to everyone who needed it.

Chapter Four

Offering Two Prescriptions: Food and Medicine

"Yesterday I diagnosed a woman with advanced HIV and probably tuberculosis, too," a medical doctor disclosed to me as we visited in Livingston, Zambia. "I was able to prescribe free antiretroviral medicine for her, but she will probably die because what she really needs are two eggs and a glass of milk. That costs fifty cents, and she will never be able to afford that much."

Two eggs and a glass of milk: a fitting reminder that if food, not just pills, were distributed to impoverished people in need, then the multibillions being expended for antiretroviral medicines could be more effectively invested by the US government, the Global Fund to Fight AIDS, Tuberculosis, and Malaria, the World Health Organization, and many national governments around the world.

When a person tests positive for HIV, ideally, medical personnel would write two prescriptions: one for necessary antiretroviral medicines and another for necessary nutrition. This does not happen in today's world, where people live on less than a dollar a day and struggle to live on one meal a day. The new global challenge is to provide a combination of free or low-cost medicine and food to impoverished people and their families in order to ensure renewed life and health.

The United Nations estimates that one-sixth of the people on antiretroviral drugs also urgently need nutritional assistance. Writing for *The Wall Street Journal*, Roger Thurow underscores the irony of getting affordable drugs to Africa without simultaneously confronting the world's highest rate of hunger. "As clinics proliferate and distribution of drugs widens," Thurow reports, "health workers are finding that hunger and malnutrition sap the therapy's effectiveness, undercutting the multibillion-dollar investments of private organizations and governments."[1]

A Model Program Is Emerging in Kenya

Kenya faces a raging HIV and AIDS pandemic. At least 5 percent of the population is infected, and 11 percent of the children are already AIDS orphans. Until recently, disease and death have stalked unimpeded through the land, and heartbreak has repeatedly triumphed over hope. Now, however, a ray of hope has broken through the clouds of despair and death, and in some places people who once lay hopeless in beds and on the floor are now walking and working again.

In eastern Kenya, in the region around Eldoret, a model program called Academic Model for Prevention and Treatment of HIV/AIDS, or AMPATH, addressing both the needs for medicine and food, has emerged. The day I visited the region, some 15,000 HIV-positive people and their families were being assisted, and each month an additional 1,000 patients were being added. Now the number being helped is over 70,000. A recent $60 million grant from the US government is designed to expand treatment to about 125,000 Kenyans.[2]

A retired sixty-six-year-old medical professor from Indiana University, Dr. Joseph Mamlin, envisioned and initiated this project in 2000. From my perspective, he is the new Albert Schweitzer of Africa, but he would be the first to reject such a comparison. However, without a doubt, the humanitarian vision, professional expertise, compassionate hearts, and persistent passion that Joe and his wife, Sarah Ellen, have embodied serve as magnets that have attracted others to be involved in this major lifesaving operation.[3]

Indiana University School of Medicine has become a partner with the Kenya government and Moi University School of Medicine to pioneer a new way of addressing hunger and antiretroviral therapies. People are now streaming into voluntary testing centers in order to get tested because for the first time there is both hope and help. Having seen family members and neighbors restored to life, they are even overcoming some of the denial and stigma that has characterized HIV and AIDS worldwide and stymied its testing and treatment.

Mamlin envisioned this project, which directs doctors to give two prescriptions: one for free medicine and another for proper nutrition. If people cannot afford nutritional food—and about one-third to one-half cannot—then they get free food for six months. Once their health improves sufficiently, they are expected to sustain themselves. Mamlin knows that if you give food to a woman with children, she likely will share most of it with her children.

Therefore, this program also uniquely provides food for every child and anyone else needing it in the family. One patient in Eldoret, Christine Kili, expressed her gratitude that her prescription for food included not only her, but also her two daughters, noting that "you can't say to your children, 'No, this is my food and I'm not sharing.' You can't eat an egg while your child has nothing."[4]

Clinicians discovered that the average patient weighed only 49 kilograms, about 108 pounds. Since, in Dr. Mamlin's words, "drugs don't have any calories," he created a comprehensive program for patients that includes food prescriptions, lessons on how to make nutritional dishes, and the development of farms and vegetable plots.[5]

The operation includes a hospital, a research center, and rural clinics, plus an agricultural component. On their four farms, they raise fruits and vegetables to supplement the food provided through the World Food Programme and the US Agency for International Development. Food assistance is provided for up to 30,000 people per month. The anti-retroviral drugs are provided through PEPFAR.

The farms also serve as teaching centers to help people learn how to improve their agricultural skills and grow necessary food for themselves and their families. Cooking lessons are provided as well as assistance in helping individuals create their own vegetable plots. The goal is to help people become self-sustaining, and thus not be forever dependent on free food. As the Welsh farmer-activist developing the farms in Kenya told me, "We literally believe in the old Chinese proverb that says, 'Give a man a fish and you feed him for a day. Teach a man to fish and you feed him for a lifetime.'"

It is unrealistic, however, to expect that medical practitioners around the world will also become successful farmers like those in Eldoret, Kenya. I agree with Marshall Matz, who argues, "While the doctor's initiative is commendable, their medical education is best used in hospitals and clinics—not in farm fields." Matz contends, "We must supplement the significant US and international effort to fight AIDS with an adequate antihunger component. Without a dedicated food-assistance program, investments to fight AIDS will not reach their maximum potential." Therefore, he proposed that future US farm bills were the proper place to initiate such a program.[6] This, together with increased funding for the World Food Programme, could make a major difference in combating both hunger and HIV/AIDS.

When tragic ethnic violence flared in Eldoret in 2008 following the disputed national election results, the Mamlins refused to leave, even when other foreigners fled. Hundreds were killed and thousands were left homeless in the nightmare of violence. At the height of the crisis, Mamlin wrote to friends:

> As far as I know, we have not lost a single AMPATH staff member or patient. Unfortunately, it is almost impossible to run clinics since there are no *matatus* [van-taxis]

running. It took almost three hours for one of our pharmacists to walk by foot to give us access to drugs. Most staff are busy securing safety of loved ones and most patients are either afraid or can't travel.

I took heart in an Emergency Room this morning when I no longer needed to step over a body...We have seen some things over the last few days that cannot be described...

[But remember,] the IU-Kenya program at its core symbolizes what is so critically needed...This is not a program dedicated to building medical schools or even stamping out a pandemic. At its heart, it is a program that screams "Yes" in a world ready to say "No." This program puts love and compassion front and center. Those values build the rest.[7]

New Life and Hope

Marshall Matz and Karen Sendleback of Friends of the World Food Programme commend the Eldoret model, saying, "With well-targeted support of medication and good nutrition, Africans can get back on their feet to confront this terrible scourge. It is an intervention that will maximize the human and material impact of the US government's great investment in fighting AIDS in Africa."

Further, they emphasize that providing food to hungry children improves not only their health, but enhances their probabilities of school attendance. These two components are mutually beneficial, as

"Evidence shows that keeping kids in school can also protect them from HIV infection."[8]

When I visited Eldoret, I met several people who had been successfully treated in this program. Like the biblical Lazarus, they had been raised from the dead. I reported on William Kahangi, the street hawker, and his journey from death to life in the first chapter. Likewise, I shall never forget my conversation with Rose, a vibrant young mother of three, who told me she, too, had been knocking on death's door. She anticipated her children soon would become orphans, as her husband had already died and there seemed no alternatives. She was alone and desperate.

But then Mamlin and his team found her and gave her needed food and medicine. Now, far from being weak and overwhelmed, she is serving as assistant manager of one of the farms. The day I saw her, this lovely young woman was bouncing across the fields, checking on the conditions of growing vegetables and fruits, seemingly as healthy and energetic as any of us visiting the farm.

Thanks to antiretroviral medicines combined with good nutrition, Rose is now a productive citizen, full of life and hope. And instead of her children languishing in some orphanage or worse yet, among the thousands of street children of Kenya, they are in school and moving ahead in life. Her story is a vivid reminder that the best way to address the global catastrophe of increasing numbers of orphans is to keep their parents alive.

But Will Indifference Prevail?

What is happening in one corner of Kenya must be replicated throughout Sub-Saharan Africa and other parts of the world. Impoverished people living with HIV and AIDS need more, not less, nutrition. Research studies under way in Kampala, Uganda, by the University of California at San Francisco and the Mbarara University of Science and Technology seek to demonstrate empirically what seems self-evident to me. Patients are being followed for two years to monitor how food insecurity impacts adherence to drug regimens, efficacy, illness, and death rates. The purpose is to show the world that "packaging food aid with HIV drugs…can actually improve health and save lives."[9]

Writing from Uganda for *The New York Times*, David Tuller, a journalist and public health graduate student, reports that "most patients I meet say they and their families scramble to survive from meal to meal, never far from the edge of starvation. Many say their HIV drugs have drastically increased their appetites and made them crave food even more." Dozens of patients were interviewed by Tuller:

> About what they eat, how much food they have, whether they grow it or buy it and whether the side effects from the medications are worse if they take the pills on an empty stomach. Our team also wants to know whether costs related to treatment limit their ability to cover basic foods and whether hunger forces women to

offer men "live sex," or intercourse without condoms, in exchange for food or money.[10]

Most American citizens cannot comprehend what it really means to be hungry or to live with food insecurity. A Burmese pastor friend of mine told me he was shocked at how often people in the United States eat chicken for dinner. On the salary he earns, he can only afford for his family to have chicken at Christmas or other very special holidays. Yet we take food abundance for granted and rarely think about what it means to have the limited choices that a peasant in India or a farmer in Africa daily must face.

In Uganda, for example, parents often face food triages, having to choose between bad versus worse alternatives. If they feed their hungry children, then they have less to sell at the market. If they don't sell enough of their harvest, then they can't afford to travel to the clinic to get the treatment they and their families need. Yet going to the clinic means losing valuable time they could have spent farming or gardening or doing other work that would have yielded desperately needed cash or helped meet their children's dietary needs. Tuller expresses his frustration at doing his social science and economics research in Uganda, saying,

I wonder sometimes what is the point of researching this? Why not just give food to people so obviously in need? But international donors demand data and documentation. They want proof that an intervention will reduce the total misery index before they will shell out millions of euros for new programs, even if the need appears self-evident.[11]

The World Food Programme continually seeks to cajole governments and nongovernmental organizations around the globe to see the link between healthy food and healthy bodies, between HIV and malnutrition, and to contribute greater nutritional resources in the battle against AIDS. Progress to date is slow, as the world community apparently has higher priorities than helping to feed the hungry and fighting the diseases that continue to inflict untold suffering upon millions and millions of people. Indifference triumphs, and offering two prescriptions, food and medicine, still remains the exception, not the rule, around the world.

The level of pain and suffering that women and children face due to the HIV and AIDS pandemic is almost unimaginable.

Children around the world are becoming the heads of households as their parents die or are too sick to care for their families. Outside Mzuzu, Malawi, I met a little nine-year-old girl, Anna. Beside her was her six-year-old sister. In a nearby mud hut with a leaky ceiling, her mother was dying from AIDS, a small baby snuggled beside her. Anna was struggling to care for all four of them. Early every morning Anna walked two miles and carried back on her head a container of fresh water. Daily she scrambled to find food from neighbors as she battled for survival.

In every small village in Malawi, I was surrounded by multitudes of orphans and vulnerable children. Near Mzuzu, my friends tried to organize an art project, but it failed because there was no room on the dirt floor for the children to put the paper down so they could draw on it. Furthermore, the children were so hungry that they nibbled on the crayons.

Impoverished women experience a high rate of illiteracy in the world. Their options for making a living are incredibly limited. If a woman's husband dies from AIDS, malaria, or tuberculosis, she often has no resources to feed her family except to sell her body by doing commercial sex work. The amount she earns is a pittance, and daily she risks violence, disease, police harassment, and public degradation.

Several times I have met with groups of these women in India, and they yearn for freedom from sexual slavery and for economic empowerment so they can feed themselves and their kids. One program the Center for the Church and Global AIDS supports has helped a number of women escape to a better life. A simple sewing machine, costing less than $100, has enabled a woman named Sudha to earn extra money to start her own business. In another case, I helped deliver monthly nutritional supplements to Harshini and her daughter—just enough to stabilize her health and keep her in a paying job so she would not have to revert to "survival sex" work.

Too often in Africa, women seeking to be self-sustaining are forced to choose between making beads for sale or selling their own bodies. The marketing of trinketlike jewelry is limited, so many females have no real choice. Needed are humanitarian entrepreneurs who will help create social businesses for women living with HIV. In Kenya I saw HIV-positive women creating malaria bed nets. A major market exists for this product. This one small group of women in the past three years has made and sold 21,427 nets.

Chapter Five

Remembering the *Olvidados* of the World: Women and Children

Some years ago, my son, Kent, spend time working with the poorest of the poor in Costa Rica, the *campesinos* who struggle for life in the rain forests. So obscure are these impoverished people that they are known as the *olvidados*, or "forgotten ones," of Costa Rica.

In the global battle against world hunger and HIV/AIDS, the primary *olvidados* of the world are women and children. Especially overlooked are the little ones who are HIV positive and those who have become AIDS orphans, having lost one or both of their parents to the disease. Each day 1,500 children worldwide become infected with HIV at birth.

When the average citizen thinks of those who are hungry in the United States, they focus on homeless men or women on skid row, since the children struggling to survive are usually invisible. Forgotten are the children who live in crowded charity shelters or broken-down urban motels, moving from location to location, school to school, each day uncertain whether there will be enough food.

The image of people living with HIV and AIDS in the United States is likewise stereotypical: in this case, gay, white, young males. Yet in reality, the overwhelming majority of people infected with HIV globally are heterosexual people of color. Nearly 50 percent are women, 60 percent in Sub-Saharan

Africa. People of all ages are infected, with millions and millions of children impacted. Every year in the United States nearly 56,300 new people are infected, 50 percent of whom are African American and more than 20 percent of whom are Hispanic. Every nine and half minutes someone new gets infected. Each year in the United States, fourteen thousand people still die of AIDS. In the age of Viagra and constant television advertising championing the eradication of erectile dysfunction, it should not be too surprising that in the United States people over fifty account for at least 10 percent of all new HIV infections.[1] Gay, white, young males still remain an endangered group, but globally, and increasingly in the United States, this dreaded disease does not demonstrate a preference solely for this sector of humanity.

Focusing on Women

The world reserves the worst stigmatization and discrimination for women. In culture after culture, country after country, religion after religion, women often are treated practically as nonpersons, relegated to second-class and third-class citizenship, subjected to violence and abuse, treated as property, limited in education and employment opportunities, and deprived of basic healthcare and reproductive information.

Women carry a disproportionate share of the burden of both the world hunger and the global AIDS pandemics. Frequently when a woman is diagnosed with HIV/AIDS, the stigmatization and discrimination is amplified and she is disowned and even abandoned. When an impoverished mother does secure food, she typically shares it with other members of the family before she eats anything herself. Often this means that she eats either no food or little food with nutritional value. The World Food Programme estimates that more than 60 percent of chronically hungry people are women.[2]

At the opening session of the sixteenth International AIDS Conference, held in Toronto, Canada, in 2006, the richest married couple in the world, Bill and Melinda Gates, called upon world leaders to "put the power to prevent HIV in the hands of women" by accelerating research on microbicides and other new HIV prevention tools. Microbicides are prevention products such as vaginal creams, gels, and capsules that would destroy harmful microbes, including HIV. Still under scientific study, user-controlled microbicides would aid in prevention but not be 100 percent effective. Field research to date has been discouraging, however, as protection proves difficult to verify and safety poses a challenge.

"We need tools that will allow women to protect themselves," said Bill Gates. "This is true whether the woman is a faithful married mother of small children or a sex worker trying to scrape out a living in a slum. No matter where she lives, who she is, or what she does—a woman should never need her partner's permission to save her own life." Melinda Gates emphasized that every life is equal and "saving lives is the highest ethical act." Boldly, she declared, "In the fight against AIDS, condoms save lives. If you oppose the distribution of condoms, something is more important to you than saving lives."[3] The Bill and Melinda Gates Foundation has made stopping AIDS the top priority of their billion-dollar donations. On the eve of the conference, they contributed an additional $500,000 to the Global Fund to Fight AIDS, Tuberculosis, and Malaria.[4]

Caregivers, Marching Grandmothers, and Circumcision

Women bear the brunt of almost all the care of orphans and provide the overwhelming majority of home-based care to people suffering with HIV and AIDS. Illustrating this inequality at the sixteenth International AIDS Conference was the colorful Grandmothers March against AIDS. One hundred African grandmothers joined a hundred Canadian grandmothers in highlighting the challenges women in particular face in the global AIDS crisis.

A panel of women from Africa, Asia, and North America noted that violence and the virus are companions. Domestic violence and rape, combined with a lack of education, female condoms, and control over their own bodies, leave young girls and women especially vulnerable to the disease. Due to the pervasive male practice of having more than one sexual partner, faithful women often get infected even though they have only had one partner. It was noted, for example, that in some parts of Africa, a woman doubles her chances of getting HIV on her wedding day.

Prevention practices for men were also highlighted in Toronto. Male circumcision may reduce the risk of contracting HIV by up to 60 percent, according to scientific studies released at the international gathering. Research by Professor Robert Bailey of the University of Illinois predicts that millions of new HIV infections could be averted in Sub-Saharan Africa if substantial proportions of men were circumcised.[5] One danger women stress, however, is that circumcised men may become even more negligent regarding condoms, somehow thinking they are HIV free because they have been circumcised.

In several candid speeches, former president Bill Clinton stressed that while "persuading boys and older men to get circumcised might be a 'hard-sell,'" every lifesaving approach must be employed. The future challenge will be convincing men that surgery can be safe, effective, and not too painful. Decisions as to how much money should be invested in providing access to this treatment have yet to be made.

No magic bullet or foolproof method exists for HIV prevention. A danger of every prevention mechanism, be it condoms, circumcision, or microbicides, remains the possibility that some people will increase their risky sexual behavior after that precaution is in place, leading to more, rather than fewer infections. Public health officials, therefore, urge education programs that emphasize both risk avoidance (abstinence, faithfulness) and risk reduction (condoms, clean needles, and circumcision).

Dr. Cristina Pimenta of Brazil noted that less than 50 percent of the world's youth have access to information about prevention. She highlighted the importance of linking prevention techniques to treatment and care, reflecting on the current tendency of the general population to see biomedical interventions as quick or magic solutions to HIV and AIDS and to devalue basic preventive measures for avoiding the disease. In many cases, especially in the developing world, those simple and effective measures are unavailable. For example, Melinda Gates noted that fewer than one in five people "at greatest risk of HIV infection have access to proven approaches like condoms, clean needles, education, and testing. That's a big reason," she said, "why we have more than 4 million new infections every year."

Raising Role and Status of Women

Stephen Lewis, United Nations special envoy for HIV/AIDS in Africa, closed the Toronto international conference by declaring that "gender inequality is driving the pandemic, and we will never subdue the gruesome force of AIDS until the rights of women become paramount in the struggle." He called for the creation of a new UN agency for women, "staffed to the teeth" and dedicated to enhancing the role and status of women worldwide. Without it, he believes that the "Millennium Development Goal of gender equality has no chance of being reached by 2015."[6]

An AIDS-free and hunger-free world will never become a reality until the social, economic, cultural, political, and religious status of women is upgraded. Women need education and skills for employment. Former US senator and presidential nominee

George S. McGovern has campaigned for a universal free lunch program, arguing that the more years of schooling a girl receives, the fewer children she tends to have and the more income she is able to earn to provide for her family. Equal human rights for all people are the key for a new world where poverty, disease, and hunger are history and humanity experiences the dawn of a new day of justice. I strongly believe that a girl without an education becomes a woman without a future.

Focusing on Children

"Let the little children starve!" "Let the little children die of AIDS before their second birthday!" No politician ever publicly makes such cruel pronouncements, but the latent consequences of national and international public policies results in an extraordinarily high death rate among children both from malnutrition and AIDS. Former Tanzanian president Julius Nyerere once asked the question, "Must we starve our children to pay our debts?" Noting the excessively heavy burden of national debt owed to the International Monetary Fund and World Bank, James Grant, former head of the UN Children's Fund (UNICEF), responded:

> Yes…hundreds of thousands of the developing world's children have given their lives to pay their countries' debts, and many millions more are still paying the interest with their malnourished minds and bodies.

Today, the heaviest burden of a decade of frenzied borrowing is falling not on the military or on those with foreign bank accounts or on those who conceived the years of waste, but on the poor who are having to do without necessities...on the women who do not have enough food to maintain their health, on the infants whose minds and bodies are not growing properly...and on the children who are being denied their only opportunity ever to go to school.[7]

One person unwilling to let the little children starve, or to be forgotten by the powerful and the rich of the world, is the unlikely prophet of the poor, the rock star Bono. He notes that it is a positive development that the public is beginning to press for action on climate change. But that urgent situation overshadows another dire sitation, one that has been ignored for some time. Bono writes:

Imagine for a moment that 10 million children were going to lose their lives next year due to earth's overheating. A state of emergency would be declared, and you would be reading about little else. Well, next year, more than 10 million children's lives will be lost unnecessarily to extreme poverty, and you'll hear very little about it. Nearly half will be on the continent of Africa, where HIV/AIDS is killing teachers faster than you can train them, and where you can witness entire villages in which the children are the parents. All over the world, countless children will die as a result of mosquito bites, dirty water, and diarrhea. It's not a natural catastrophe—it's a completely avoidable one.[8]

Alert: Child Killers on the Loose

Malnutrition remains the number-one child killer in the world. One child dies every five seconds from hunger and starvation, but in our minds they are only numbers, not names, and facts, not faces.[9] Of the more than 1 billion people living in extreme poverty in the world—more than the populations of the United States, Canada, and the European Union combined—350 million or more are children.[10] Five hundred twenty-four million of the world's hungry live in southern Asia; that's more than the populations of Australia and the United States.[11]

Children worldwide are victims of violence, viruses, and vicious malnutrition. Widespread physical abuse of children by family members, acquaintances, and soldiers is alarming. Reports of child sexual abuse in some countries borders on 30 percent. The Global AIDS Alliance indicates that "nearly 50 percent of all sexual assaults in the world are committed against girls aged 15 years or younger." In Malawi, studies discovered 50 percent of school-aged girls had been sexually assaulted by teachers or male classmates.[12] Displaced women and children, who make up 80 percent of the world's refugees and internally displaced people, are especially vulnerable to violence and rape.[13]

UNICEF estimates that 10.9 million children under age five die in developing countries each year, 60 percent due to malnutrition and hunger-related deaths.[14] Nearly 5 million children die each year from preventable diseases such as diarrhea and measles. An estimated 684,000 deaths of children could be prevented yearly by increasing access to vitamin A and zinc. Lack of vitamin A weakens the immune system and causes child blindness. UNICEF contends that iron deficiency, the most common form of malnutrition, is impairing the mental development of 40 to 60 percent of the children in developing countries.[15] And every minute, a child under the age of fifteen dies of an AIDS-related illness and yet another child becomes HIV positive.[16]

Babies get infected by HIV in three ways: either in the womb, upon delivery, or during breast-feeding. If a woman receives antiretroviral prophylaxis during pregnancy and delivery and the infant gets this medicine shortly after birth, the probability of the mother passing the HIV infection to her baby is sharply reduced. UNICEF claims significant progress in reducing the rate of mother-to-child transmission. In 2005, only 11 percent of women living with HIV were getting drugs to prevent transmission. In 2008, 31 percent were estimated to be receiving treatment.[17]

HIV-positive women face a tragic dilemma. An infant runs a risk of getting HIV from breast milk.

However, eliminating breast-feeding increases the baby's risk of a diarrheal disease, respiratory illness, malnutrition, or death because of unclean water. Formula-feeding is expensive, and even if it is affordable and safe, it may prove problematic because family members and neighbors may suspect that mothers who are formula-feeding are HIV positive and therefore stigmatize them. Since 2006 UN agencies have recognized that mothers have to make choices based on their own individual and cultural circumstances. In general, the recommendation is to breast-feed exclusively for the first six months of life, unless formula-feeding is "acceptable, feasible, affordable, sustainable, and safe" for both mother and infants.[18] For the impoverished woman and child, meeting all of these five criteria proves nearly impossible.

Every Child Left Behind

Even as world leaders began to talk about "access for all" in terms of antiretroviral treatments for HIV and AIDS, the underlying reality is that "all" rarely includes children. The disease has already ravaged many young lives. UNICEF reported in 2008 that:

> For millions of children, HIV and AIDS have starkly altered the experience of growing up. In 2007, it was estimated that 2.1 million children under age 15 were living with HIV. As of 2005, more than 15 million children under 18 have lost one or both parents to AIDS. Millions more have experienced deepening

poverty, school dropout and discrimination as
a result of the epidemic.[19]

Age-appropriate antiretroviral medicine has not
been readily available for children. Only a very small
proportion, probably 5 percent of the children needing treatment for HIV and AIDS, has received it. Very
slowly, AIDS pediatric care has increased, from 70,000
children in 2005 to 127,000 in 2006. Children in the
developing, or two-thirds, world have been deemed
expendable by pharmaceutical companies, international programs, and even their own governments.

Children especially illustrate the incredible
importance of linking food and medicine together.
Even if antiretroviral medicines were available to
them, clearly malnourished children could not tolerate powerful dosages. Babies have no extra bodily
resources to handle medicine; they need nutritious
food and clean water simultaneously with age-
appropriate medicine.

In an AIDS pediatric center in Namakkal,
India, I came face to face with the injustice being
perpetrated on impoverished children of the world.
A British pediatrician was explaining to the children
and parents gathered in a small room how they must
attempt to cut an adult-size pill into three exact por-
tions. If a child is too young or too sick to swallow it,
then the pill must be crushed and absorbed in water.
Liquid medicine for children is generally not available, and existing medicines often are foul-tasting
and children understandably spit them out.

As I stood there in the room with perspiration flowing from my brows, I was both disheartened and outraged. How in the world were these mothers and fathers, who live in crudely made huts often stuck together with cow manure, going to cut the pills? How could they find consistently clean water to mix with the crushed medicine? And even if they did succeed, no assurance exists that the particular portion of the pill, which was crushed, might not contain too much toxic substance. If you take a whole pill, all the elements are sufficiently blended, but consuming only one-third enhances risks and may cause more illness, not less.

I realized as I stood in this little clinic room that unless the global powers that be chose to reverse their priorities and rush to production new and generic medicines designed especially for the young, the world has pronounced a death sentence on these beautiful children. At that very moment, I realized the little ones around me were probably doomed to an early death. "No child left behind" might be a popular political motto in the United States, but when it comes to hungry and sick children in the developing world, our unspoken slogan is "Every child left behind." In 2009—almost thirty years since the pandemic began—a fixed-dose generic pediatric anti-retroviral combination drug was approved by the World Health Organization and the US Food and Drug Administration. The reality remains that most children worldwide with HIV and AIDS die by the age of five; 50 percent never see a second birthday.

Children everywhere embody hope. When we asked children in an Indian AIDS orphanage the question "What do you want to be when you grow up?" they answered with familiar responses: teacher, pilot, doctor, policeman, and so on. But my fear is they will never grow up, as they will not get the necessary medicine, care, food, and education needed.

In Zambia I saw a roomful of cribs with orphans aged one month to six months and another with babies aged seven months to a year. Twins Peter and Paul lay beside each other with little staff attention. One little child peered at me with such hope and fear that the bars of his crib seemed like a prison. Almost no one in the world wants to adopt a baby with HIV or AIDS.

Nowhere is the situation more grim for children than in the Congo. Indeed, these little ones are the *olvidados* of Africa. Death is on a vast and cataclysmic scale, as the child mortality rate in the eastern provinces is almost twice as high as it is in the rest of Sub-Saharan Africa, which already has the world's highest rate. Thirty thousand children there were forced into military militias, and unfathomable numbers of girls were raped during the constant civil conflicts. Lydia Polgreen of *The New York Times* reports that "orphans choke the streets of Kinshasa, the capital, bedraggled platoons in Congo's vast army of want." She says that "this is how the crisis in the Congo kills, with the most banal weapons: a gauntlet of hunger and disease that…kills one in four children before the age of 5." After describing the gruesome death of two-year-old Amuri from untreated measles, she writes:

> The day Amuri died of measles, a boy sick with a treatable respiratory infection died, and so did an infant with tetanus, another easily preventable disease. The day before, it was malnutrition and malaria that stole two young lives…A child dies in Congo almost every two minutes, mostly from preventable causes.[20]

Focusing on Ourselves

Does anybody give a shit? This is the same perplexing dilemma posed in the initial chapter of this book. After examining the fate of humanity's *olvidados*, we must ask whether the pandemic of global indifference will ultimately triumph.

This question haunts me: do I really care? I once asked a young man from Goshen, Indiana, whether his family and friends understood why he continued to work long hours in an orphanage in Chiang Mai, Thailand. "No," he said, "because if they understood, they would start to care, and if you start caring, then you have to act. They probably would rather not know." Knowing, caring, acting: a trilogy most of us would rather avoid.

Christians are easily embarrassed by talk about condoms. Historically, Roman Catholic teaching has condemned their use, claiming it was unnatural family planning. Protestants generally have endorsed family planning but hesitate to promote condoms for fear it leads to promiscuity.

At an Asian conference of pastors from many countries and denominations, I spoke about the need for HIV prevention and pulled a condom package out of my pocket. After I sat down, a woman physician from Taiwan lectured next. She declared it wasn't enough to simply display a package—it needed to be opened and a demonstration given. As the audience nodded in agreement, she declared most of them had never seen a condom, because they feared going to the store to buy one lest people would stigmatize or gossip about them.

In Kenya at a seminar for pastors and spouses, a woman asked to empty a bag could only giggle and was too embarrassed to share what was inside. The next volunteer displayed the dildo and condom inside, but when he was asked to show the proper way of using a condom, he did not know how. Finally, a woman pastor came forward and gave a full demonstration. Not only did Kenyans not know how to use a condom, but of the seven men, age eighteen to sixty-eight, from the US participating, I was the only one who had ever seen a condom tutorial. For all the AIDS education emphasis on the "correct and consistent use of condoms," a major gap in knowledge and practice exists globally.

Chapter Six

Thank God for Condoms

For many people, far worse than a clergyman using profanity is a religious leader advocating condoms. Nothing strikes greater surprise—and sometimes elicits hostility and reveals hypocrisy—than when a padre promotes the correct and consistent use of condoms. Yet I feel like I have little choice if I want to work toward an AIDS-free world.

Unlike malnutrition, which can be cured with appropriate and regular nutrition, HIV and AIDS are incurable diseases, and prevention is the only recourse available to avoid its spread. With 33.4 million people in the world currently HIV positive, and with the numbers increasing daily, one would hope that religious groups and leaders would be on the front lines of the prevention battle. Unfortunately, this is rarely the case.

Religion can play a significant role in both encouraging and discouraging HIV and AIDS prevention. Religious beliefs, attitudes, teachings, and practices can contribute both negative and positive dimensions to efforts aimed at promoting HIV and AIDS prevention. Unfortunately, religious leaders and groups have contributed to the spread of HIV and AIDS by their attitudes and actions.

Papal Opposition to Condoms

One great stumbling block in preventing HIV and AIDS has been the voice of the Vatican, and of the pope in particular. While Roman Catholics are to be commended for having been on the forefront of compassionate and noble responses for care and treatment, their leadership has failed miserably in the arena of promoting prevention.

Vatican theologians have long opposed artificial contraception. In contrast, Protestant theological thinkers support planning parenthood and believe that sex is a gift from God and meant for pleasure, not just procreation. Many Protestant pastors tend to be wary, however, of freely advocating condom use, since they fear it promotes promiscuity among the unmarried.

The official Roman Catholic position regarding condom use has often mistakenly been interpreted as the only or definitive perspective within the Christian community. In reality, Protestant teachings differ significantly from Catholic, and the Roman Catholic faith community proves to be diverse in its thinking and practice. At an AIDS orphanage I visited in Cambodia, for instance, the priest and nuns in charge shunned talking about condoms, but the public health information they distributed clearly demonstrated how condoms were to be properly used.

Noted for his conservative theology, Pope Benedict XVI had been relatively silent about condom use after being elevated to the papacy. However, in 2009, en route to Cameroon on his first trip to Africa, he alarmed AIDS advocates worldwide with his astonishing, unexplained claim that "one cannot overcome the problem with the distribution of condoms. On the contrary, they increase the problem."[1]

Clearly, condoms alone cannot stop the pandemic; numerous prevention methods are required, including promoting abstinence, being faithful to partners, ensuring gender equality, considering circumcision, developing microbicides, and exercising self-discipline. But by distorting the scientific evidence in favor of his own theological preferences, Benedict invited an overwhelming chorus of criticism. *The New York Times* editorialized that the pope "has every right to express his opposition to the use of condoms on moral grounds," but "he deserves no credence when he distorts scientific findings about the value of condoms in slowing the spread of the AIDS virus."[2]

More pointed was the *Lancet* editorial that lamented manipulating science to support Catholic ideology. The editors contend that when "any influential person, be it a religious or political leader, makes a false scientific statement that could be devastating to the health of millions of people, they should retract or correct the public record." By not doing so, Benedict XVI has done an immense disservice "to the public and health advocates, including many thousands of Catholics, who work tirelessly to try and prevent the spread of HIV/AIDS worldwide."[3]

Fortunately, there are some rare and brave Roman Catholic leaders who speak in opposition to the papal message. In Cameroon, Cardinal Christian Wiyghan Tumi declared, "If a partner in a marriage is infected with HIV, the use of condoms makes sense." Bishop Januário Torgal Mendes Ferreira of Portugal says, "I have no doubt that…prohibiting condoms is to consent to the death of many people."[4]

Professor Edward Green of Harvard University wrote in *The Washington Post* that "The Pope may be right," saying there is evidence that "condoms have not worked as a primary intervention in the population-wide epidemics of Africa." Those who have used condoms in Africa have tended to engage in even riskier sexual behavior because they have a false trust in the efficacy of condoms and do not use them correctly or consistently. Men who have multiple concurrent sexual partners have driven the pandemic in Africa. Therefore, Green concludes that any decline in HIV infection rates in Africa came about not from condom promotion, but for other reasons such as "zero grazing" (sticking to one partner). Green argues, "Condoms cannot address challenges that remain critical in Africa, such as cross-generational sex, gender inequality" and ending "domestic violence, rape, and sexual coercion." Unlike the pope, Green is not anticondom, acknowledging that "condom promotion has worked in countries such as Thailand and Cambodia."[5]

Idealism versus Realism

Thank God for condoms! Imagine for a moment how many people in the world might now be infected if it were not for the protection they provide. A British poster proclaims, "Condoms are the world's best weapons of mass protection." Without them, the world would be left nearly defenseless in this global pandemic. I prefer a theology of condoms rather than coffins.

All sexual activity involves a degree of risk; there is no safe sex, only safer sex. Condoms are not 100 percent reliable, but when used consistently and correctly, they have an exceptionally high rate of effectiveness. Condoms are a necessary, if not a sufficient, strategy for ending AIDS in the world. As Yale theologian Margaret A. Farley notes, the use of condoms in stopping the virus "has nothing to do with a contraceptive goal; it has only to do with preventing people from dying."[6]

From an ideal or religious perspective, all people would develop such depths of character that they could restrain from risky sexual behavior for the rest of their lives. This proves problematic even for close-knit, supervised priestly communities whose members have made pledges of abstinence and are submerged in rituals designed to enable them to fulfill this special gift of chastity or sexual purity. The advocacy of such an unrealistic approach for older teenagers, young adults, and others in the Viagra era is almost beyond comprehension.

Believing all humanity is going to subscribe to the church's ideal of no sexual intercourse except in marriage is neither realistic nor intelligent. CNN commentator Roland S. Martin notes that on that subject, the pope faces up to realities of risk and self-preservation. Martin writes:

> Pope Benedict surely loves God and sees him as his protector and provider, but he goes nowhere

without armed bodyguards. The pope has to know that murder is against God's will. He has to believe that every person has the choice to be a moral and upstanding person. Yet not everyone abides by those religious views and his security is there to prevent him from being harmed. So how are condoms any different?[7]

Advocates of abstinence and anticondom crusaders generally do not feel that the immediacy or urgency of the AIDS pandemic should influence their teaching or approach. They think condom advocacy undermines the moral principles they proclaim and that careful, patient, thorough, responsible education will be persuasive enough to maintain a commitment to abstinence. They are willing to risk the dangers to people on an individual and mass scale in order to preserve their religious or political standards. Others would deem that approach immoral as we think that shows a careless disregard of probable consequences. To reiterate the words of Melinda Gates, "In the fight against AIDS, condoms save lives. If you oppose the distribution of condoms, something is more important to you than saving lives."[8]

Other Opponents of Condoms

Lest I be misunderstood, the pope is not the only religious stumbling block to HIV and AIDS prevention. Many other religious leaders and communities of faith have set up major obstacles to block effective efforts. Just as politics is often accused of creating strange bedfellows, the campaign against HIV and AIDS has often been composed of an unusual, if not strange, coalition of bedfellows: orthodox Roman Catholics, right-wing evangelicals, and conservative Muslims. The latent consequence of silent and apathetic mainline Protestant leaders in regard to HIV has likewise resulted in less emphasis on prevention.

Public health officials and nongovernmental agencies often despair of working with religious groups because of their insistence on abstinence-only rather than comprehensive evidence-based prevention programs. Even when the United Nations was preparing in special session to declare HIV and AIDS a global emergency, a coalition of predominately Roman Catholic and Muslim nations rejected the measure because of strong opposition to promoting condom use. During the presidency of George W. Bush, abstinence-only policies had strong backing from his religious conservative core of political supporters.

Politicians likewise are often blinded by their ideologies. For thirteen years—until early 2009—Dallas County, Texas, banned free condom distribution because the commissioners court believed it encouraged "illegal and immoral behavior." This impractical policy contributed to Dallas County having the highest HIV/AIDS prevalence in the state of Texas. The 35 percent increase in the number of HIV-positive people over the last five years, including a tripling of the rate among people age thirteen to twenty-four, finally prompted a three-to-two vote authorizing the county health department to distribute no-cost condoms.[9]

From the very beginning of the AIDS pandemic, condoms have sparked controversy. President Ronald Reagan's surgeon general, C. Everett Koop, astounded both his political and religious supporters when he advocated condom use. He later remarked it was not easy for him as a sixty-five-year-old man, a husband, father, and grandfather "to become known as the 'Condom King.'" He noted, however, that he "could not in good conscience exclude anything that saves lives. I was Surgeon General of the United States, not the chaplain of the United States."[10]

Zambia's first president and one of Africa's greatest independence leaders, Dr. Kenneth Kaunda, lost a son to AIDS in 1986. Kaunda says many think he lost his Christian faith and morals when he began promoting condom use to fight AIDS. Some church leaders claimed he had only pretended to be a Christian and now was teaching people how to misbehave. Kaunda's reply was:

> Dear friends, thank you for what you're saying, but remember this: among those we have lost are Reverends, Priests, Fathers, Sisters and many others in church work. If you had not preached against the use of condoms, those people might have been alive today. Now they're six feet down and you can't help them. If they'd used condoms, they might have been alive, and you would have been able to help them spiritually to recover.[11]

UNAIDS has set forth a series of principles to guide effective HIV prevention. The emphasis is that all prevention efforts and programs must fundamentally promote, protect, and respect human rights, including gender equality. Scientific evidence, not ideology or theology, should steer public policy. While approaches may differ among social and cultural groups, the key commitment is that HIV prevention is for life, not death, and every effort needs to be made to reduce the possibilities of HIV infections.[12]

What People of Faith Can Do

People of faith, regardless of their religious affiliation, need to recognize how restrictive or judgmental religious tenets and tendencies can complicate efforts to eradicate the disease. Conversely, they need to discern how theological and ethical convictions combined with compassion can contribute to protecting the well-being of people and promote the goal of an AIDS-free world. Faith communities and individuals can become stepping stones, contributing positively to prevention programs and becoming partners in the struggle to conquer HIV and AIDS.

Some religious leaders, for various reasons, may never find it possible to speak openly about all means of prevention, especially condoms. But that does not mean they cannot find other ways of becoming prevention advocates. For example, at a temple outside of Chiang Mai, Thailand, I met with a Buddhist abbot who has become an AIDS activist. In his rural region, HIV infections and AIDS deaths have mounted. I asked him if he ever spoke about condoms when he addressed the topic of prevention. He smiled, quickly saying, "Never. But I always have a public health nurse speak immediately after me."

In the battle against AIDS, many a public health advocate is grateful if the religious leaders simply stay out of the way and do not create barriers or blockade efforts to stymie the infection. In a best-case scenario, religious leaders work together in partnership with health advocates to protect the health of the community.

While the discussion of condoms epitomizes the tension in prevention efforts, other issues also prevail. Religious leaders in various parts of the world have felt that nongovernment and government organizations have been too ready to endorse sexual freedom without giving appropriate attention to the importance of encouraging abstinence among youth, including delayed sexual debuts, and championing fidelity between partners. In some African cultures young people start having sex by the age of twelve; each year this debut can be delayed the probability of infection is reduced. Having unprotected sex with multiple sexual partners also increases the risk of infection. Thus, campaigns that stress all three letters of the alphabet of life—*A* for *abstinence*, *B* for *being faithful*, and *C* for *condoms*—increase the possibilities of health, not disease, and life, not death.

Campaigns against sexual violence and sexual slavery can provide a basis for partnership between religious and secular groups committed to combating

HIV and AIDS. As long as gender inequity prevails in a society, controlling and combating HIV and AIDS becomes a greater challenge. Women are biologically more susceptible to the virus, and when they lack control over their own bodies, they are vulnerable to infection from their husbands or other male partners. Religious patriarchal thinking must be challenged since it often reinforces cultural machismo, making women highly exposed and legally defenseless.

"If Allah had meant for us [women] to ask questions, he would have made us men." This shocking statement opens the movie *Brick Road*, based on the novel of the same name by Monica Ali.[13] A young Bangladeshi girl, Nazneen, is being silenced from asking questions about life and death, being told instead to learn to accept her fate as a woman in today's world.

Is it inevitable fate or the will of God that everywhere on earth women suffer the greatest stigmatization and discrimination for having HIV and AIDS? In country after country women are denied basic human rights, blamed for the pandemic, and experience poorer medical care.

Is it fate or divine will that women are classified as second-class citizens not only in society, but in their faith communities? Women are biologically, culturally, economically, and religiously more susceptible to HIV. Should they simply accept their fate and endure the status quo as the numbers of women infected and affected by HIV and AIDS rise dramatically around the world?

Would men remain silent and passive if this were happening to them? Would they think it natural if women failed to join with them in changing trends that are infecting and killing more and more of their gender year by year? Would men think they were simply destined to die, even though conditions could change if personal attitudes and political will were altered?

The resounding answer to all of these questions is no. Men would not accept inequality as the norm of human society and personal relationships. They would protest that it is neither inevitable fate nor divine will but the sinful human propensity for injustice. They would speak out against human rules and customs that stigmatize and dehumanize their gender. They would argue that culture, not Christ, is controlling the rules of their religious communities. They would rebel, organize, strategize, and fight for life against death, and they would call upon their sisters to join them in this revolution.

AIDS Prevention Focused on Women

Women are raising profound questions, and men should be joining them to challenge established social mores and conventional religious traditions that contribute to the HIV and AIDS pandemic. A major contribution of faith-based leaders and communities to creating an AIDS-free world would be to join government and nongovernmental efforts focusing on women and prevention. Women are particularly imperiled by the anticondom champions. Let me enumerate just a few of the dilemmas they face.

First, what is a married woman to do if her husband is HIV positive? The being faithful (also known as zero grazing) part of the ABC approach to AIDS prevention is a Russian roulette experience for her: every time she has sexual intercourse with her partner, she risks becoming infected. Surely, nearly thirty years into the pandemic one would think conscientious religious leaders from the smallest parish to the Vatican would be trumpeting exceptions and exemptions for married couples to the no-condom policy, but tragically only muffled voices are heard and elaborate theological casuistry persists.

For example, in Uganda 76 percent of all new infections are sexually transmitted, and of all new infections, 42 percent occur during marital sex. Obviously Ugandan wives have reason to fear being intimate with their husbands, yet they have had no access to female condoms in this country. Advocates are hoping to introduce them in the fall of 2009.[14]

Second, macho male attitudes resist condom use. In Africa men boldly declare that "you don't eat a banana with the peeling on" or "you don't suck on candy still in the wrapper." Whether you are in South America or southern Asia, you are likely to hear men claiming that using a condom reduces sexual pleasure. An advertisement aimed at African American men in South Carolina tackles this macho attitude by showing a bevy of pills that a person with HIV may have to take and asking the question, "What is a greater bother—taking 12 pills or using a condom?" In South Africa a man told me rather proudly that his attitude and behavior was changing: he now used a condom with his mistress but not his wife. No wonder married women are considered endangered species in the global AIDS crisis!

In religious circles around the world, I find it is chiefly men who are most opposed to condoms for so-called moral reasons. Remember, it is men who, over the centuries, have developed the theological rationales to justify why condoms should not be used, and it is primarily men who speak out in both Roman Catholic and conservative Protestant circles to condemn condoms today.

Male insecurity, embarrassment, and hypocrisy about talking about condoms are nearly universal. Yet in the United States, every family sporting event seems to be sponsored by the pharmaceutical companies focused on recreational sex and selling products to ensure erections and ejaculation, though we use the euphemism "erectile dysfunction" and try to leave the kids wondering what the product really does. Some suggest even the serious warning about "consulting a doctor if an erection lasts more than four hours" is really a clever marketing ploy. In contrast, condoms are still rarely advertised on mainstream television, and when they are, a public outcry often erupts.

I passed around a condom to pastors at an AIDS seminar in Cambodia; I swear they would have been more comfortable handling a machine gun. In Oklahoma the response was not much different. On the first day of an AIDS conference in Lusaka, Zambia, for Presbyterian and reformed pastors, every male speaker's reference to condom use was negative. So I decided to push the envelope a bit the next day, and I flashed a condom packet during my speech on prevention. But a Zambian woman in the back row decided to push me a bit and hollered out, "Are you going to open it?" Lest I appear to be an unmanly coward, I hesitatingly opened the condom and did a little demonstration on my thumb—noting, of course, that if you only put it on your thumb, you can't prevent an HIV infection. Amazingly, the audience relaxed after a bit of nervous laughter, then became more honest and human, and never again did the nattering nabobs of negativism surface in the presentations.

Third, female condoms remain nearly inaccessible. Even though men have a record of resisting condom use, women have been left with no option. Most women in the world, including well-educated professional females in the United States, have never seen, much less used a condom created just for their gender, though they have been available since 1992 in Europe and since 1993 in the United States. Because male condoms are less expensive, both government and nongovernment organizations have not made the female alternative available to the masses.

Nearly thirty years into the AIDS pandemic, reliance has been overwhelmingly tilted toward the male condom. In 2008, *10 billion* male condoms were distributed versus *35 million* female condoms.[15]

In Africa, where 60 percent of all HIV-infected people are women, female condoms have been very rare. A Johns Hopkins University study showed that 10,000 HIV cases could probably be prevented in South Africa if 16.6 million female condoms were distributed, with a $35.7 million savings in health-care costs.[16] Aaron Motsoaledi, the new health minister, decided in 2009 to double the number of free condoms. Free male condoms will increase from 283 million to 450 million by 2010, and by an additional 45 million in the following fiscal year. However, female condoms will only increase from 4.5 million to 5 million, a figure far from 16.6 million proposed by Professor David Holtgrave at Johns Hopkins.[17]

Available in Asia for the past ten years, female condoms have been distributed at a rate of less than 1 million for a population of at least 1 billion women of reproductive age. Because they were first promoted to female sex workers in Thailand and Vietnam, female condoms became stigmatized among many. In Indonesia, efforts were stymied both by a strong patriarchal culture opposed to any condom use and by their high cost.[18]

A second-generation female condom produced by the Female Health Company was approved by the US Food and Drug Administration in 2009 and should be about 30 percent less expensive. The first-generation version costs between $1.15 and $2.75 in the United States and from $.80 to $2.10 in other countries. This price has made female condoms prohibitively expensive for most women in a world where many people earn less than $1 a day. The hope is for global distribution to reach 50 million yearly so that costs can drop as low as $.25.

Fourth, women with HIV and AIDS experience a high level of stigmatization and discrimination. People around the world report that even worse than having the disease is the way they are treated. If a person is hungry and malnourished, people tend to respond with compassion and care. They do not immediately start asking questions such as Did you spend your money foolishly? Did you fail to plant crops? What did you do wrong to make God punish you with starvation? People diagnosed as HIV positive must be prepared to have their morals questioned and to experience discriminatory treatment, both personally and among their family members.

Infected women often discover that they are accused of being commercial sex workers and then thrown out of their homes, even when they have been infected by their husbands. Domestic violence is rampant toward HIV-positive women in Africa, Asia, and Latin America. Scorned by friends and extended family members, the women live in terror, uncertain how to cope with the illness and its consequences.

Religious groups, including the church, bear great responsibility for contributing to this stigma and discrimination. Moralistic and judgmental, the church and its leadership have often been quick to label people as sinners and suggest they deserve their plight. In reality, most women in the world with AIDS are far more sinned against than sinners themselves, since they have borne the brunt of illiteracy, hunger, poverty, disease, unemployment, and gender inequality.

Male church leaders in particular should confess their complicity in supporting stigmatization and discrimination and act with contrition. At the religious preconference preceding the seventeenth International AIDS Conference, held in Mexico City in 2008, Lutheran bishop Mark Hanson knelt and washed the feet of two women as a public act of repentance for the church's shaming and shunning HIV-positive people around the world.

The two women earlier had shared their experiences of gender violence, human trafficking, and mistreatment by church communities. Herlyn Maja Uiras of Nambia told how she was raped when she was fourteen and illegally transported out of her country. Sophia of Mexico noted that in "many countries, just being a woman is dangerous" due to machismo attitudes and violent behavior.

Hanson, the presiding bishop of the Evangelical Lutheran Church in America and president of the Lutheran World Federation, challenged the church to break its silence about gender violence and to create safe places for women. "We male religious leaders must reexamine our theology and practices," said Hanson, "and act humbly before persons infected and affected by HIV and AIDS."

Overcoming Complacency and Indifference

These four dilemmas are illustrative of the problems being experienced by women in the world, especially those who are impoverished and illiterate. Instead of endless condom controversies, the primary emphasis should be on addressing poverty and overcoming the indifference that keeps people from actively promoting HIV and AIDS prevention for both men and women.

Even more of a hindrance to wiping out AIDS than religious leaders fearful of sex and wedded to dysfunctional theologies is our human propensity for complacency and indifference. As the economist Adam Smith centuries ago noted, most of us can read about a global crisis, be it famine wiping out millions or a health crisis, and yet head for bed and snore peacefully through the night. Yet if we knew our little finger was slated for amputation the next day, we would spend the night tossing and turning.[19]

Why?

How can we make a difference in the world? Twice, people have given me money before I have gone abroad, telling me to use it to help some person in need. Once I gave $300 to a Baptist woman evangelist who told me she had gone to convert the people in their homes but discovered many of the women had been tossed out because they were HIV positive due to their husbands' infections. They now were encamped outside the walls of the city, and she wanted to reach out to them and their children with a program of nutrition and healthcare. Another time, in Bangladesh, I gave money to a youth pastor who used it to help a young woman get tested for HIV and to provide her with professional counseling aimed at changing her risky sexual behavior. Small gifts may not change the world, but they can certainly improve the world of particular individuals.

A woman in Zambia began to realize how many children were in need because they were suffering from AIDS and malnutrition, but she had no training and no resources to help them. About the same time, a British man came to Livingston to see the magnificent Victoria Falls and to enjoy a safari. When he returned to London, he apparently offered a prayer of thanksgiving to God for his safe journey. To his surprise, he heard a voice saying, "And what did you do for the people of Zambia?" Reluctantly, he admitted his indifference by saying "Nothing." He then had a vision of a short woman trying to start an orphanage. So a few months later, he returned to Livingston. At the tourist *office he asked if they knew a short woman who was starting an orphanage. They found her, and the man provided the first $20,000 to initiate a much-needed AIDS orphanage.*

chapter Seven

Conquering Indifference

Since the early 1990s, with John Guare's play and a subsequent movie, most of us have been acquainted with the idea that there may be only six degrees of separation between us and any other person on earth.

I was reminded of the phenomena when the tragic events of Virginia Tech unfolded and we learned that thirty-two students had been murdered. Initially, I thought I had no connection to that campus, but soon I learned that the boyfriend of my nephew's daughter was studying there. And then the shocking news came that two of my grandniece's best friends, Erin Peterson and Reema Samaha, had been brutally killed. This nightmare in American history was only two relationships away from me; my family was connected to the tragic pain and terrible suffering.

More Than Six Degrees of Separation

However, there appear to be more than six degrees separating most of us from the poorest of the poor in the world. Every three seconds a person dies somewhere in the world due to poverty—8 million nameless people a year. One billion people go to bed hungry every night. Last year 2 million people died of AIDS and almost 3 million became infected with HIV. In the United States we spend about $6,000 per person each year on healthcare, compared with $20 or less per person in Sub-Saharan Africa.[1] The moral, religious, and political scandal of people dying from hunger and diseases in a world with enough food and medicine for all hardly causes a ripple in the consciousness of most people.

A published op-ed piece in *The Denver Post* recently illustrated our tendency toward self-indulgence. Writer T. J. Wihera frankly described the lifestyle and choices most of us make. He audaciously said that he loves his dog more than he loves any person. He would therefore rather pay $1,000 to help his pet survive diabetes than offer $5 to charity. Describing the costs of veterinarian visits, syringes, insulin, vitamins, blood-clotting tests, and so forth, he bluntly announced:

> This is privileged treatment compared to what I am willing to give most people, including those starving in Third World countries. If someone were to show up at my door tomorrow asking for $1,000 to save the life of some faraway person, I wouldn't bat an eye before shaking my head and shutting the door.
>
> And that has little to do with the amount of money. In a quick Internet search, I found organizations that say one can feed a starving person for as little as 8 to 14 cents per day. That's a maximum of $51.10 per year for a human life. But I'm not ponying up.

Making himself clear, he wrote that rather than save the life of a person, "even if I could prevent [his death] with $51.50…I'd rather pay for the dog's insulin than for some faraway person's food."[2]

Why do we face such massive indifference? Is this young man the exception or the rule in American society today? Besides the exceptional humanitarian, do most of us continue our normal routines of life with little or no sense of the plight of enormous numbers of human beings globally? We know there are people in the world who are desperately hungry and sick, but why do we permit this knowledge to break through to our conscience for only very limited periods? Do all of us love our dogs more than the world's impoverished?

Moving from the mind to the heart, from *thinking* about global AIDS and world hunger to really *caring* about people, proves to be the first, and perhaps the longest, step in the journey away from indifference. We all know the statistics, but I wonder what this young Denver journalist would think if he came with me to Africa or Asia. What if he came face to face with the suffering child, the dying widow, the broken man? Would he still love his dog more than any of these human beings? If he were up close and personal with extreme poverty, would he not want to help? Would he not feel some remorse about the gigantic gap between the rich and poor?

Addressing the Challenge of Indifference

Psychologist Harriet Lerner addresses the challenge of indifference. She notes that psychologists have diagnostic labels for overreactions, such as *hypochondria*, *social phobia*, *panic disorder*, and *post-traumatic stress disorder*, but missing are "similar diagnostic labels for folks who fail to get anxious when they should." She bemoans the fact that many ordinary citizens go about their business as usual, without responding to "dangerous, unfair, or downward spiraling events in their families, communities or global environment." When it comes to problem solving, she notes that "when anxiety disrupts functioning, it is considered a psychiatric illness," but "there is no diagnosis for indifference, the most dangerous emotion of all."[3]

Humanity is equipped to deal with immediate threats to our own well-being: through fear and anxiety. They are natural survival mechanisms that warn us "to keep the door shut when the wolf is waiting outside, or prime us to fight, flee or freeze when the wolf has found his way in. In the face of imminent danger, we need to react—not stop and ponder the pros and cons," according to Lerner. What we often cannot recognize are crumbling and threatening circumstances outside our daily sphere, since we often have no clear personal warning signs alerting us to them and to the complications or consequences of our indifference. Letting poverty and disease spiral endlessly out of control behind the totalitarian "bamboo curtain" of Burma (Myanmar), for example, seems no threat to most of us. But if someday diseased birds start flying across that border and the dreaded avian flu starts encircling the earth, then we will question whether our self-interested perspectives were far too shortsighted. Out of sight and out of mind describes both the global AIDS and world hunger crises—and that is exactly how many citizens want them to be.

Fortunately, however, a new wave of national and international concern is rolling across the earth. This chapter seeks to outline a few of these trends.

The Power of Individuals

First is the power of an individual to make a difference. The French writer Romain Rolland has defined a hero as "someone who does what he can." Marshall Matz contends our heroic challenge is "to do what we can—to do all we can—in the global fight" to end hunger and global AIDS.[4]

People around the world are stepping forward and indicating they want to do something about earth's wretchedness. Every day, heroes are emerging in almost every community as people of all ages band together in volunteer labor. Retired people have chosen to give back what they received by working with orphans in South Africa, or water projects in India, or development projects in Bolivia. Rock star Bono has initiated the ONE campaign, which has effectively mobilized the best hopes and dreams of more than 2 million Americans into advocacy and action. They are "united in the belief that where you live should no longer determine whether you live."[5]

Columnist David Brooks describes these modern do-gooders as social entrepreneurs who are neither saints nor socialists, as in previous generations, but often venture capitalists who "are almost will-fully blind to ideological issues." That means:

> Aside from the occasional passion for heir-loom vegetables, they are not particularly crunchy. They don't wear ponytails, tattoos, or Birkenstocks. They don't devote any energy to countercultural personal style, unless you consider excessive niceness a subversive fash-ion statement. Next to them, Barack Obama looks like Abbie Hoffman.

Instead, "they are data-driven and account-ability-oriented," and "they've got spreadsheets, and they want to save the world." Not interested in work-ing for big, sluggish bureaucracies, "they are not hos-tile to the alphabet-soup agencies that grew out of the New Deal and the Great Society; they just aren't inspired by them."[6]

Counting himself among those do-gooders, Bono has recognized the incongruity of his rich life-style with his passion for speaking for justice and equality. In forum after forum he has worked in a bipartisan fashion to wipe out unforgiven national debts, spoken to the powerful in high government places about poverty and hunger, and pressed people to face the global AIDS crisis. In a famous National Prayer Breakfast, he confronted both President George W. Bush and Congress with a theology that probably made them twist. Bono proclaimed a God of justice, not charity, declaring:

God may well be with us in our mansions on the hill. I hope so. He may well be with us in all manner of controversial stuff. Maybe, maybe not. But the one thing we can all agree, all faiths and ideologies, is that God is with the vulnerable and poor.

God is in the slums, in the cardboard boxes where the poor play house. God is in the silence of a mother who has infected her child with a virus that will end both their lives. God is in the cries heard above the rubble of war. God is in the debris of wasted opportunity and lives, and God is with us if we are with them.[7]

During my speaking tours in the United States and abroad, I am impressed by increasing numbers of people who are discovering the power one individual has to make a difference. This power of hope has a ripple effect on others as individuals make sacrificial commitments, speak out against stigma, urge business and professional leaders to get involved, advocate public policies that have major financial implications for good, and raise funds in their schools, offices, service clubs, churches, synagogues, temples, and mosques.

The Power of Organizations

Mother Teresa championed the power of one, often proclaiming that she could not save the whole world, but "one by one by one" she could make a difference. Of course, she didn't simply rely on her own individual initiative. More a saint than a social entrepreneur, Mother Teresa succeeded in inspiring others to partner with her, mobilizing a dedicated organization called the Missionaries of Charity that continues her work today around the world.

An explosion of new charitable organizations has emerged in recent years as people have sought to funnel their ideas, energies, and financial resources into the battles against poverty, hunger, and disease. In his book *Giving: How Each of Us Can Change the World*, former president Bill Clinton illustrates how individuals have created effective and compassionate organizations that are saving lives and solving problems around the world. Clinton asserts that "we all have the capacity to do great things" and "citizen activism and service can be a powerful agent of change in the world."[8]

Clinton noted that after completing fulfilling careers, many people are discovering new life by devoting themselves to humanitarian endeavors. Personally, after twenty-nine years as a college and seminary president, I have experienced a renaissance of life by engaging in the struggle to end hunger and AIDS in the world. By creating a nonprofit 501(c)(3) charity, the Center for the Church and Global AIDS, I have been able to challenge individuals and faith-based communities to change their behavior regarding HIV and AIDS from condemnation to compassion, stigmatization to liberation, and apathy to action. Our focus is to support and advocate for people infected and affected by HIV and AIDS in the world through programs of education, prevention, care, and treatment.

As I have traveled and lectured extensively in the United States, I have found people of all ages eager to get involved. What many appreciate about my own organization is that the overhead is almost nonexistent, so their dollars go directly and quickly to the intended project. While almost all want to contribute financially, many want to volunteer their services either to help the organization or to go directly to Africa, Asia, or Latin America to be of service in an AIDS orphanage, a feeding program, or in direct work experiences digging wells, laying bricks, teaching students, or caring for the sick.

Working toward the attainment of the Millennium Development Goals (MDGs) outlined in the first chapter has to be a priority of government, but government alone cannot achieve these objectives. Nongovernmental organizations of all types are imperative for the successful implementation of policies and programs. For example, fighting the stigma attached to HIV and AIDS ultimately becomes an effort that must be addressed on an individual-by-individual and community-by-community basis. Massive government programs can fail if prejudice prevails against the ill and impoverished.

Because people want answers to the question What can I do? I often conclude lectures on HIV and AIDS with a quick list of possibilities. Number one is always to encourage people to protect themselves against the virus, and second is to be sure their loved ones have the necessary knowledge for prevention. As an elderly lady in South Africa told me, "Knowledge is power, and our people have been deprived of that power." If we care about protecting ourselves and our families, then surely we want to ensure that others have the knowledge and choice of how to prevent infection.

Possible opportunities for involvement are innumerable. What is important is that everyone explore ways to make a difference in the world. Many civic and faith-based charities exist that effectively share their resources with the world's neediest. Getting involved with these organizations provides a way to marshal resources and talent toward the solutions of problems, even problems such as world hunger and global AIDS that are seemingly intractable.

Additionally, a critical need exists for citizens to be engaged in public policy advocacy that addresses issues like world hunger and global AIDS. Politicians need to know that citizens care about food stamp programs and international aid projects. When I asked former senator and Republican presidential nominee Bob Dole what he thought the role of faith-based organizations should be in regard to domestic and international hunger, I expected him to respond that they should run food pantries and kitchens. Instead, his first response was that churches should be lobbyists for Africa, because unless they spoke out for the poorest of the poor, nobody else would. Organizations like Bread for the World and the Global AIDS Alliance play a significant role in helping to mobilize the average citizen to become a champion of improved public policies.

The Power of Governments

As a result of a new level of citizen conscience-raising, governments are beginning to slowly move toward greater social equity and justice, particularly in regard to global AIDS and world hunger. Yet the gap between individual and nongovernmental organizational initiatives and the US government response still remains substantial.

Jeffrey Sachs, a Columbia University economist, notes that efforts of individuals and nongovernment organizations are essential in that they "are world-changing when they point to new strategies, approaches, and technologies that can then be taken to scale through government support and partnership." Pointing to AIDS pioneer Dr. Paul Farmer, who demonstrated that impoverished people in Haiti loved life so much that they could be trusted to follow complicated drug regimens, Sachs underscores that it takes major government funding to sustain strategies and ideas through programs like PEPFAR and the Global Fund to Fight AIDS, Tuberculosis, and Malaria.[9]

The US government has never fully embraced the MDGs. Critics claim they are overly ambitious and flawed; yet they remain the first and only existing international framework for reducing global poverty.[10] In specific areas like HIV and AIDS, the United States has led the global battle, but in other areas results have been mixed. For example, promoting gender equality and women's empowerment is not a US policy or spending priority. Military might, not ending poverty, is our highest priority, as evidenced by yearly spending of $499 billion for the military and $22.7 billion for foreign aid.[11]

InterAction, a coalition of 165 US-based international nongovernment organizations focusing on the world's poor and most vulnerable people, has issued a critical and comprehensive report called *US Contributions to Reducing Global Poverty: An Assessment of the US and the Millennium Development Goals*. It notes that official development assistance (ODA) from the United States has increased in recent years due to PEPFAR and the Millennium Challenge Corporation (which is concentrated on infrastructure improvement and economic growth), but development assistance to many countries in Africa and Latin America for health and education has actually diminished.

National security rather than humanitarian aid to the poor has dictated the US response. The five countries receiving the bulk of assistance are Israel, Egypt, Afghanistan, Iraq, and Pakistan. The poorest countries of the world have been left behind. The United States has focused specifically on AIDS and malaria—a vertical approach to poverty—rather than the more comprehensive approach envisioned by the MDGs. More than twenty-six US government agencies are involved in foreign assistance, and critics contend there are no unifying goals or country-level coordination.[12]

For the past sixty years, the United States has been the leading donor of ODA, but the global development community argues that a percentage of the gross national income, not volume of money given, best measures a nation's contribution to addressing global poverty, hunger, and disease. Wealthy countries in 2000 generally agreed to increase annual foreign aid for development to 0.7 percent of their gross domestic product (GDP) by 2015. The United States falls far short of that goal, ranking twenty-first in the list of the twenty-two top donor countries.

Currently, less than 1 percent of the US budget goes to humanitarian concerns. Bono and other international aid advocates argue that the United States should direct at least an additional 1 percent of the US budget toward meeting basic needs and fighting poverty in impoverished companies. Albert Reynolds notes that:

> What an additional 1 percent of the federal budget means in terms of percent GDP is that an increase of 1 percent, combined with the 0.7 percent of the federal budget we now give for development, would be the equivalent of around 0.4 percent of our GDP. This would raise the US to a percent of GDP that would be comparable to the European Union.[13]

The United States has been the world's largest provider of food, giving more than 340 million metric tons of US agricultural commodities over the past fifty years. But InterAction and Bread for the World contend that:

> The US has no overarching approach or strategy for reducing global hunger or preventing it in the long term. Our food-assistance programs respond to the immediate needs of recipients, saving lives and reducing malnutrition, but do not address the underlying causes of their hunger and, therefore, cannot contribute to halving hunger in the long term.[14]

Sending surplus food abroad is costly to Americans and often undercuts local economies and does not meet long-term needs. Needed is a cash-based food-assistance program so that local crops, including fresh fruits and vegetables, can be purchased. Current political realities in the United States, however, have prohibited policy makers from moving in that direction, partly in fear that ultimately the United States will send neither cash nor commodities.[15]

Hunger is escalating rapidly around the world. In 2008 prices of basic staples—corn, wheat, rice—reached record highs, up 50 percent or more in a six-month period. Causing this phenomenon have been rising demands, droughts, and high costs of oil, making transporting food and purchasing fertilizer more expensive. Additionally, greater reliance on biofuels has resulted in less food for human consumption. The secretary-general of the United Nations, Ban Ki-moon, calls this "the new face of hunger, increasingly affecting communities that had previously been protected. Inevitably, it is the 'bottom billion' who are hit hardest: people living on one dollar a day or less." He does not despair, however, of meeting the MDG of halving the number of hungry by 2015.[16]

Ki-moon urges greater humanitarian outreach, noting the need for greater governmental support of the World Food Programme, which fed 102 million people in seventy-eight countries in 2008 (including 3 million daily in Darfur). Among his specific recommendations are to initiate school meal programs at a cost of less than $.25 a day. The underfunded McGovern-Dole International Food for Education and Child Nutrition Program serves as an excellent model for creating a global school lunch program. It addresses not only the issue of hunger, but also encourages young girls and women to stay in school, with the consequence of fewer pregnancies, less HIV/AIDS, and greater national social and economic development.[17] On a more comprehensive scale, Ki-moon promotes improving market efficiency and increased agricultural production, envisioning a green revolution like Asia experienced in previous decades.[18]

As the initial PEPFAR legislation came up for renewal in 2008, Congress, acting in a bipartisan fashion, sought to keep up the promise of universal access to HIV and AIDS prevention, care, and treatment by providing $48 billion by 2013. About $9 billion of the $48 billion will be focused on fighting malaria and tuberculosis. The goal is to increase the number of people receiving antiretroviral treatment for HIV and AIDS to 3 million (including 450,000 children), provide medical and nonmedical care for 12 million people (including 5 million orphans), and train at least 140,000 new healthcare workers before 2013.[19]

Unless the United States wants to be responsible for a new genocide, the government has no real option for discontinuing its AIDS foreign assistance in the future. To cut off funding for antiretroviral drugs would prompt catastrophic results, with near certain death for those dependent on US-funded medicine. Possibilities for an effective HIV vaccine remain as distant a dream as at the beginning of the pandemic almost thirty years ago. Trial test after trial test fails, even though the National Institutes of Health spent $497 million in 2008 for vaccine research.[20] The ABC prevention approach (*abstinence, being faithful,* and *using condoms*) will continually need to be stressed, along with adding additional letters representing the alphabet of life, such as *D* for *development, E* for *gender equality,* and *F* for *food.*

Overcoming Global Attention Deficit Disorder

Many Americans are afflicted with what journalist David Sarasohn calls "Africa Attention Deficit Disorder." We get momentarily engaged in the AIDS crisis in Sub-Saharan Africa, starvation in Ethiopia, or poverty in Sierra Leone, but quickly these tragedies disappear from our daily radar screens. "The real problem with our AADD," says Sarasohn, "is that the people who have it aren't the ones who suffer from it."[21]

Overcoming this global attention deficit disorder or American amnesia proves to be as challenging as finding an HIV vaccine or eliminating hunger in the world. Yet signs are promising, as more people seem to sense that being a citizen requires more than loyalty to a nation, but also a global perspective in an interconnected world. When confronted by staggering statistics suggesting that one-fifth of the world's population suffers extreme poverty, despair about doing anything to make a difference can easily become victorious. Yet a generation ago one-third of the world population fell into that category, so despite population growth, the plight of humanity has been improving, thanks to the intentional humanitarian efforts of individuals, nongovernmental organizations, and governments.

Stephen Lewis, former UN secretary-general Kofi Annan's special envoy for HIV and AIDS in Africa, wrestled with despair and frustration in the face of the human carnage he experienced. Faced with bureaucratic inertia and personal heartbreak, he has watched millions perish, yet he remains a hopeful man. While he strives to make major changes in governmental policies, he takes solace and has gained strength from small achievements. While knowing the mind-boggling statistics of hunger and AIDS, he still feels the transforming power of individual stories and quests for a better life.

Names, not just numbers, enabled him early in the twenty-first century to alert the world to the holocaust sweeping the African continent. He became a leading advocate and interpreter encouraging the United Nations, governments, and individuals to act. Personally, Lewis reports, "I've come to the point where it is as though saving one human life is what it's all about. In the beginning, there were these huge numbers and you wanted to drive everything forward. Now I think, 'Can we somehow save those five lives in Zanzibar? Can we somehow keep those 10 people alive in Malawi?'"

At times I, too, despair and think my work in vain. But then my spirit of hope and confidence is revived again when I meet someone whose life has been saved or changed thanks to compassion without borders. In Zambia it was a beautiful young professional woman, Anna, who stood up after I finished speaking and thanked me for speaking out openly and boldly before a conservative religious audience about the necessity of preventing HIV by consistently and correctly using condoms. In northeast India it was a middle-aged man, Kumar, who thanked me for breaking the conspiracy of silence by confronting the evils of stigma and discrimination. In Burma it was the urgent request of young couples sitting on a dirt floor, sharing water and bread with me and pleading that I must speak for them because they had no way to advocate for themselves. In Malawi it was in the faces of young children waiting eagerly for hours for a few pieces of food and a drink of juice. In southern India, it was Bojo, who didn't ask for anything to help him overcome his illness and hunger, but simply said, "Thank you for being my friend."

There is no way to forget those faces or erase those names from my mind. As more and more fellow citizens come to understand and experience the interconnectedness of humanity and begin to feel their anxiety and anguish, the chances increase that indifference will recede and compassion will triumph. Conquering indifference is not inevitable, but neither is it impossible.

Endnotes

Chapter One: Beyond Nameless Numbers

1. Associated Press, "UN: World Hunger Reaches 1 Billion Mark," June 19, 2009. See also "1.02B Chronically Hungry People Worldwide, UN Says," *Financial Times*, June 19, 2009.
2. Jeffrey D. Sachs, *The End of Poverty* (New York: Penguin Books, 2005), 18.
3. Available at www.bread.org/learn/hunger-basics/hunger-facts-international.html (accessed November 14, 2007).
4. Ibid.
5. Cindy Patton, *Globalizing AIDS* (Minneapolis: Univ. of Minnesota Press, 2002), 31.

Chapter Two: The Faces of Global HIV and AIDS

1. Kofi Annan, opening statement, International Partnership against HIV/AIDS in Africa conference, New York City, December 6–7, 1999. Annan has repeated this perspective and phrase in many speeches.
2. UNAIDS, "09 AIDS Epidemic Update," see http://data.unaids.org/pub/Report/2009/JC1700_Epi_Update_2009_en.pdf.
3. *The Next Wave of HIV/AIDS: Nigeria, Ethiopia, Russia, India, and China* (Washington, DC: National Intelligence Council, 2002), 4.
4. See World Bank, as reported by Reuters, "HIV/AIDS Treatment and Prevention in India: Costs and Consequences of Policy Options," *Yahoo! News*, August 13, 2004. http://site resources.worldbank.org/INTINDIA/Resources/IndiaART Report1.pdf.
5. Richard Feachem, *AP/Seattle Post-Intelligencer*, September 15, 2004, www.kaisernetwork.org/daily_reports/rep_index.cfm?DR_ID=25766.
6. Bill Gates, "Slowing the Spread of AIDS in India," *The New York Times*, November 9, 2002. Available at www.nytimes.com/2002/11/09/opinion/09GATE.html.
7. MAP report, *AIDS in Asia: Face the Facts*, 2004. Available at www.fhi.org/en/hivaids/pub/survreports/aids_in_asia.htm#.

Chapter Three: World Hunger: Cause and Consequence of Global AIDS

1. Reported by Cade Fields-Gardner of Cary, Illinois, in an address during the George McGovern Conference at Dakota Wesleyan University, Mitchell, SD, November 2005.

2. The Global Fund, *Partners in Impact—Results Report 2007*. Available at www.theglobalfund.org/en/publications/pro gressreports/?lang=en.

3. See "Global Fund Releases Figures on Progress of HIV/AIDS, Malaria, TB Programs Ahead of G8 Summit," Kaiser Daily HIV/AIDS Report, May 23, 2007. Available at www.kaiser-network.org/daily_reports/rep_index.cfm?DR_ID=45085.

4. "*Economist* Examines Progress of WHO's 3 by 5 Initiative," *The Body: The Complete HIV/AIDS Resource*, April 3, 2006. Available at www.thebody.com/content/art7993.html (accessed May 24, 2007).

5. Ibid.

6. The United States President's Emergency Plan for AIDS Relief, Background. Available at www.pepfar.gov/pepfar/guidance/76828.htm (accessed November 17, 2007).

7. Ibid., Latest Results. Available at www.pepfar.gov/about/c19785.htm (accessed November 17, 2007).

8. See "Bush Announced Request for $30B, Five-Year Extension for PEPFAR," Kaiser Daily HIV/AIDS Report, May 31, 2007. Available at www.kaisernetwork.org/daily_reports/rep_index.cfm?hint=1&DR_ID=45249.

9. President George W. Bush, State of the Union Address, February 28, 2008.

10. David Beckmann, "Bread for the World Responds to 2008 State of the Union Address," News Release, January 28, 2008. Available at www.bread.org/press-room/releases/bread-for-the-world-responds-to-2008-state-of-the-union-address.html.

11. Neil MacFarQuhar, "Experts Worry as Population and Hunger Grow," *The New York Times*, October 22, 2009. Available at www.nytimes.com/2009/10/22/world/22food.html.

12. "US Food Aid Policy to Be More Flexible, Clinton, Vilsack Say," Kaiser Daily Global Health Policy Report, October 20, 2009.

Available at http://globalhealth.kff.org/Daily-Reports/2009/October/20/GH-101009-US-Food-Aid.aspx.

13. Gerald J. Stine, *AIDS Update 2007* (New York: McGraw Hill, 2007), vi.

14. Judy Wollen, "Hope and Help in Africa Asked and Answered: Efraim Kabaija, Chief of Staff to President Paul Kagame of the Republic of Rwanda," *World Ark* (Heifer International magazine) July/August 2006: 34. Available at www.heifer.org/aids.

15. "What Does a Cow Have to Do With HIV/AIDS Relief?" Heifer International brochure.

16. See George McGovern, Bob Dole, and Donald E. Messer, *Ending Hunger Now: A Challenge to Persons of Faith* (Minneapolis: Fortress Press, 2004), 8.

Chapter Four: Offering Two Prescriptions: Food and Medicine

1. Roger Thurow, "In Kenya, AIDS Therapy Includes Fresh Vegetables," *The Wall Street Journal*, March 28, 2007.

2. Shari Rudavsky and Daniel Lee, "$60 M to Help IU Fight AIDS/HIV," *The Indianapolis Star*, November 20, 2007.

3. For more details about this model program, see Fran Quigley, *Walking Together, Walking Far: How a US and African Medical School Partnership Is Winning the Fight Against HIV/AIDS* (Bloomington: Indiana Univ. Press, 2009).

4. Thurow, "In Kenya, AIDS Therapy Includes Fresh Vegetables."

5. Marshall Matz and Karen Sendelback, "Nutrition Vital in AIDS Battle," *The Denver Post*, June 9, 2006.

6. Marshall Matz, "Eliminating Hunger Is Today's Moral Imperative," *Des Moines Register*, October 17, 2006.

7. E-mail circulating among friends and supporters from Dr. Joseph Mamlin, January 2, 2008.

8. Marshall Matz and Karen Sendelback, "Prescription for AIDS Zone: Food Plus Medicine," *The Indianapolis Star*, October 23, 2005, E3.

9. David Tuller, "Food Scarcity and HIV Interwoven in Uganda," *The New York Times*, December 25, 2007.

10. Ibid.

11. Ibid.

Chapter Five: Remembering the *Olvidados* of the World: Women and Children

1. Lucille Scott, "Getting On (And Off)," *POZ*, April 2007, 20.

2. See website for World Food Programme, www.wfp.org, and Food and Agricultural Organization of the United Nations, *The State of Food Insecurity in the World, 2006: Eradicating World Hunger—Taking Stock Ten Years after the World Food Summit* available at www.fao.org/docrep/009/a0750e/a0750e00.HTM.

3. Marilyn Chase, "Melinda Gates Tops the List," *The Wall Street Journal*, November 20, 2006.

4. I attended the sixteenth International AIDS Conference, held in Toronto, Canada, in August 2006. Quotations are from presentations I heard there. See also Lawrence K. Altman, "A Familiar Pair Urge Greater Attention for AIDS," *The New York Times*, August 15, 2006, and the Kaiser Daily HIV/AIDS Report for August 22, 2006. Available at www.nytimes.com/2006/08/15/world/americas/15aids.html.

5. Male circumcision dates back to at least 2300 BC in Egypt. Today about 30 percent of men in the world are circumcised; 67 percent in Africa. HIV circumcision-related studies have been conducted in Uganda, Kenya, South Africa, Malawi, Zambia, and the United States.

6. See Stephen Lewis, *Race against Time: Searching for Hope in AIDS-Ravaged Africa*, 2nd ed. (Toronto: House of Anansi Press, 2005), 112–144.

7. James Grant, cited in the 1989 UNICEF "State of the World's Children" report in Lewis, *Race against Time*, 24.

8. Bono, "Guest Editor's Letter," *Vanity Fair*, July 2007, 32.

9. See Food and Agricultural Organization of the United Nations, *The State of Food Insecurity in the World, 2006*.

10. Ibid.

11. Ibid.

12. "Zero Tolerance: Stop the Violence against Women and Children, Stop HIV/AIDS," Report, Global AIDS Alliance, August 1, 2006, 5. Available at http://aidsalliance.3cdn.net/

cfbfc372c0ec68f29d_sgm6b8q7z.pdf.

13. See Women's Commission for Refugee Women and Children, "Women's Commission Fact Sheet," 2006. Available at www.womenscomission.org.

14. See World Food Programme, www.wfp.org/content/statement-conference-foreign-affairs-committee-chairpersons-eu-parliaments-paris-france-220708.

15. UNICEF, *Vitamin and Mineral Deficiency: A Global Progress Report*, 2. Available at www.micronutrient.org/CMFiles/PubLib/VMd-GPR-English1KWW-3242008-4681.pdf.

16. World Food Programme HIV/AIDS Unit, 2007. See http://one.wfp.org/aboutwfp/facts/index.asp?section=1&sub_section=5.

17. UNICEF, *Children and AIDS: Second Stocktaking Report*, 2008, 5. Available at www.unicef.org/publications/files/ChildrenAIDS_SecondStocktakingReport.pdf.

18. Ibid., 9.

19. Ibid., 2.

20. Lydia Polgreen, "War's Chaos Steals Congo's Young by the Millions," *The New York Times*, July 30, 2006.

Chapter Six: Thank God for Condoms

1. Quoted in John Thavis, "Pope's Condom Comments Latest Chapter in Sensitive Church Discussion," Catholic News Service, March 17, 2009. Available at www.catholicnews.com/data/stories/cns/0901232.htm.

2. Editorial, "The Pope on Condoms and AIDS," *The New York Times*, March 17, 2009.

3. Editorial, *The Lancet*, March 8, 2009. Also noted in Kaiser Daily HIV/AIDS Report, March 27, 2009, available at www.kaiserhealthnews.org/Daily-Reports/2009/March/27/dr00057723.aspx.

4. John M. Buchanan, editorial, "The Case for Condoms," *The Christian Century*, June 2, 2009, 3.

5. Edward C. Green, "The Pope May Be Right," *The Washington Post*, March 29, 2009, A15.

6. Margaret A. Farley, "Prophetic Discourse in a Time of

AIDS," in *HIV Prevention: A Global Theological Conversation*, ed. Gillian Paterson (Geneva: Ecumenical Advocacy Alliance, 2009), 67. See also James F. Keenan, ed., *Catholic Ethics and HIV/AIDS Prevention* (New York: Continuum, 2002) for more information.

7. Roland S. Martin, "Commentary: Pope Wrong on Condoms," March 18, 2009. Available at www.cnn.com/2009/POLITICS/03/18/martin.condoms/index.html.

8. Marilyn Chase, "Melinda Gates Tops the List," *The Wall Street Journal*, November 20, 2006.

9. See "Officials in Dallas County, Texas, Lift Condom Distribution Ban," Kaiser Daily HIV/AIDS Report, January 15, 2009. Available at www.kaisernetwork.org/daily_reports/rep_index.cfm?DR_ID=56460.

10. C. Everett Koop, cited from *Christianity Today* in Peter Gill, *The Politics of AIDS: How They Turned a Disease into a Diaster* (New Delhi: Viva Books, 2007), 15.

11. Kenneth Kaunda, cited from *Christianity Today* in Gill, *The Politics of AIDS*, 125–126.

12. UNAIDS, "Intensifying HIV Prevention," Policy Position Paper, 2005. Available at http://data.unaids.org/publications/irc-pub06/jc1165-intensif_hiv-newstyle_en.pdf.

13. See Monica Ali, *Brick Lane* (New York: Scribner, 2003) and the movie by the same name, released in 2008.

14. Serra Sippel, "Uganda to Reintroduce Female Condoms," June 29, 2009. Available at http://rhrealitycheck.org/node/10572.

15. "AP/Long Island *Newsday* Examines New Female Condom," Kaiser Daily HIV/AIDS Report, April 20, 2009. Available at www.kaisernetwork.org/Daily_Reports/rep_index.cfm?DR_ID=58093.

16. Editorial, "Female Condom Will 'Benefit' Public Health, Women Worldwide," *Chicago Tribune*, January 27, 2009. Also noted in Kaiser Daily HIV/AIDS Report, available at www.kaisernetwork.org/Daily_reports/rep_index.cfm?DR_ID=56632.

17. Caiphus Kgosana, "Minister Doubles Condom Distribution,"

July 1, 2009. Available at www.iol.co.za/index.php?set_id=1&click_id=125&art_id=vn20090701113933284C428017.

18. Ramona Vijeyarasa, "Female Condom Access, Use Low in Asia-Pacific," February 24, 2009. Available at http://rhrealitycheck.org/print/9355.

19. Adam Smith, *The Theory of Moral Sentiments* (1759; repr., Eastford, CT: Martino Fine Books, 2009).

Chapter Seven: Conquering Indifference

1. Nina Munk, "Jeffrey Sachs's $200 Billion Dream," *Vanity Fair*, July 2007, 143.

2. T. J. Wihera, "I Love My Dog More Than You," *The Denver Post*, February 17, 2008, E1.

3. Harriett Lerner, *The Dance of Fear* (New York: Harper Collins, 2004), 52.

4. Marshall Matz, "Eliminating Hunger Is Today's Moral Imperative," *Des Moines Register*, October 17, 2006.

5. Bono, "National Prayer Breakfast," in *Bono: On The Move* (Nashville, TN: Thomas Nelson, 2006), 29.

6. David Brooks, "Thoroughly Modern Do-Gooders," *The New York Times*, May 21, 2008.

7. Bono, *Bono*, 18.

8. See Bill Clinton, *Giving: How Each of Us Can Change the World* (New York: Alfred A. Knopf, 2007) for more information.

9. Jeffrey Sachs, "Something's Gotta Give," *Fortune*, September 18, 2007.

10. See, for example, "The Eight Commandments" and "Are We Nearly There Yet?" in *The Economist*, July 7, 2007, 25–28 and 12–13.

11. Munk, "Jeffrey Sachs's $200 Billion Dream," 146.

12. See *US Contributions to Reducing Global Poverty: An Assessment of the US and the Millennium Development Goals* (Washington, DC: InterAction, 2007), 6–8.

13. Albert Reynolds, "The United Nations Millennium Development Goals and Their Relationship to the ONE Campaign," 2007. Unpublished paper used by permission.

14. *US Contributions to Reducing Global Poverty*, 29.

15. Ibid.

16. Ban Ki-moon, "The New Face of Hunger," *The Washington Post*, March 12, 2008, A19.

17. See George McGovern, Bob Dole, and Donald E. Messer, *Ending Hunger Now: A Challenge to Persons of Faith* (Minneapolis: Fortress Press, 2005), 71–75.

18. Ban Ki-moon, "The New Face of Hunger."

19. David Brown, "Pact Would Give Global AIDS Fight Triple the Money," *The Washington Post*, February 28, 2008, A1.

20. David Brown, "AIDS Vaccine Testing at Crossroads," *The Washington Post*, March 26, 2008, A4.

21. Cited in "Century Marks: American Amnesia," *The Christian Century*, September 6, 2005, 6.

Index

About the Author

Donald E. Messer, executive director of the Center for the Church and Global AIDS, is the former president of Dakota Wesleyan University and president emeritus of the Iliff School of Theology, in Denver, Colorado. He has traveled extensively in Asia, Africa, and South America, speaking on issues related to the hunger and AIDS crises. He is international chair of the United Methodist Global AIDS Fund Committee.

He was honored by the US Jaycees in 1975 as one of America's Ten Outstanding Young Men. He received Alumnus of the Year awards from both Boston University and Dakota Wesleyan University. In 2005 Messer received a Lifetime Achievement Award from the Tamil Nadu Dr. M.G.R. Medical University in Chennai, India, and in 2008 he was named to the South Dakota Hall of Fame. In 2009 he received the Community Partner Award from the Hispanic Sisters of Color United for Education, in Denver, Colorado.

Author of fifteen books, his previous volumes included *Breaking the Conspiracy of Silence: Christian Churches and the Global AIDS Crisis*, *52 Ways to Create an AIDS-Free World*, and *Ending Hunger Now* (coauthored with former senators George McGovern and Bob Dole).

He and his wife, Bonnie, reside in Centennial, Colorado, are the parents of two children, and have five grandchildren. For more information about the author and his work, visit www.churchandglobalaids.org.